JOHN M. BOREK

DAVID

from
SHEPHERD
to
SOVEREIGN

21ST CENTURY
PRESS
PUBLISHING WITH PURPOSE
WWW.21STCENTURYPRESS.COM

DAVID:
FROM SHEPHERD TO SOVEREIGN

President, Liberty University
Lynchburg, Virginia

Published by 21st Century Press
Springfield, MO 65807

ISBN 0-9749811-0-9

Cover: Keith Locke
Book Design: Terry White

Visit our web-site at: 21stcenturypress.com
and 21stcenturybooks.com

For childrens books visit: sonshippress.com
and sonshipbooks.com

21ST CENTURY
PRESS
PUBLISHING WITH PURPOSE
WWW.21STCENTURYPRESS.COM

DEDICATION

Without the guidance of the Holy Spirit and the support and encouragement of my family, this book would not have been possible. I dedicate this book to my wife Lois - thank you for 40 wonderful years by my side; to my girls, Rebecca, Catherine, and Jennifer, for the joy you bring to my life; to my son-in-laws, for caring for my girls and my grandchildren; and to my seven grandchildren for reminding me of the truly important matters in life.

Acknowledgements

My pastor, Dr. Jerry Falwell, consistently challenges me to seek the heart of God and serve Him alone; Dr. Harold Wilmington, Dr. Dan Mitchell and Dean Elmer Towns, who have guided me in seeing the great truths contained in the Scriptures and in following biblical doctrines; Dr. Danny Lovett, who constantly encourages me to memorize and apply God's Word to my life; my assistant Sharon Hartless, who daily enables me to successfully lead Liberty University with confidence; Jana Verstraete, who diligently edited several versions of the text; Jamie Quetglez, who typed and compiled many segments of the manuscript; and Pastor Doug Porter, who has assisted in the production of this book every step of the way.

CONTENTS

Without a doubt, David was the greatest king to ever rule Israel. He was the king by which all others were measured. The pages that follow look at several defining moments in David's life in the context of the unique struggles he faced as he grew from shepherd to sovereign, the principles that helped him make it to the top, and what it took to stay there.

When Samuel arrived to anoint a king among the sons of Jesse, no one even thought of David. His father lobbied for the job to go to one of his seven older brothers. David was not even invited to the ceremony. But while others had overlooked the young boy, God looked closely and spotted the heart of a king. (See I Samuel 16:7)

At age seventeen, David came face to face with Goliath, the Philistine champion that even the king refused to fight. Some thought that David was ill-equipped for the task, but the lessons learned as a shepherd became foundational to his success as a soldier. Some may consider David's victory as military, but the defeat of Goliath was a spiritual victory. (See Ephesians 6:10)

Young David was promoted quickly and given great prestige after defeating Goliath, but his success exposed a jealous streak in King Saul. The reigning monarch responded with ridicule, interference aimed at blocking his continued success, and attempts to prematurely end David's life. David not only survived this work environment, he refused to let the hostile conditions hinder him in accomplishing his goals.

Jonathan was the best friend a man could ever have. Enraged with David's success and full of hatred, Saul actively sought to destroy David. Jonathan, Saul's son and David's friend, found himself involved in a unique dilemma. He responded by risking everything to intercede on behalf of his friend.

There was no quick solution to David's struggles with Saul. Rather, the principles that governed his daily actions for more than a decade resulted in David's survival, and can result in a similar victory when consistently applied to life today, even when the days are dark and the years grow long.

Despite the news of the death of his adversary, Saul, David's problems were not over. Only part of the nation of Israel invited him to be their king. By continuing to practice the principles that elevated him as king over Judah, he prepared for the day when he would serve the entire nation as their king.

As king of all Israel, David felt it was time to move the ark of God to his new capital. This seemed like a good plan at the time, but it proved to be the wrong plan in God's eyes. David finally achieved his goal when he set aside his personal agenda to do things God's way. Others may not have understood his enthusiasm at the time, but God knew his heart.

More than anything else in life, David wanted to build a temple for

God. Even the prophet thought it was a good idea. But God said no. To David, this just didn't seem fair. But in dealing with the death of his dream, David discovered a different dream, an even greater dream, that God wanted him to pursue.

After years of struggle, David finally reached the zenith of his career. This was the time when he could finally get even with those who had cost him so much anguish. But instead, he showed gratitude to Mephibosheth, choosing to forgive the sins of his grandfather and remembering the assistance of his father years earlier. It was not the usual sort of behavior of kings, but David was not the usual sort of king. (See Ephesians 4:32)

The problem with success is that sometimes it makes a person start believing their own press releases and begin thinking they are invincible. David thought that he had gotten away with concealing his sin with Bathsheba. But God still knew what was going on and sent Nathan to David with a difficult message. Nathan found a creative way to make the King listen to a message he really didn't want to hear. (See Numbers 32:23)

As if life wasn't bad enough already, David was on the run, having to flee his own capital because his own son had threatened his life. He was on his way back into the wilderness where he had spent so many years so long ago. The last thing he needed to hear was Shimei's unsolicited criticism. But the way David handled his critics illustrates an effective way to deal with the criticism of others. (See Matthew 5:44)

Sooner or later, even the greatest kings pass on and others assume their thrones. David was barely still alive. It had been a long time since he had led the nation into battle and his frail body could not survive much longer. Adonijah's attempt to usurp the throne proved that the time had come to do the last great act of kings. The principles David used to guide Solomon into assuming his father's throne set a pattern for all leaders. (See 2 Timothy 2:1, 2)

Several descriptions of a great leader are highlighted throughout the book as they become evident in the life of David. This appendix gathers them together, serving as a checklist by which leaders can evaluate their own leadership qualities.

INTRODUCTION

Why read another book on leadership?

David was the greatest leader to ever rule Israel. He became the standard by which all other kings have been measured. What better person to look to for guidance than King David, a revered leader among men and a man after God's own heart (Acts 13:22)?

David lived a long life, rising from a simple shepherd alone in the field to the leader of God's chosen people. Fortunately, the Bible records his life, providing fertile ground for analysis. His psalms and the recordings of Samuel detail many physical and spiritual victories as David overcame hostile conditions to become one of the most influential leaders of all time. The Bible and time leave no doubt that he was more than a leader. He was a great leader.

As he lived a life of triumphs and failures, David always turned to God for wisdom and forgiveness. His character and the quality of his triumphs were clearly founded on his relationship with God.

His life journey reveals principles for great leadership and his example provides key elements for a successful journey through life. His legacy challenges current and future leaders in all professions to distinguish themselves among others and to follow the heart of God.

CHAPTER ONE

WHEN FRIENDS AND FAMILY IGNORE YOU

1 Samuel 16:1-13; Psalms 8:1-9; 19:1-14; 23:1-6

Alone again. Sometimes that seemed like the story of his life. In the distance he could see the small village he called home and could tell from the din of noise echoing across the valley there was some kind of celebration taking place. He could only imagine the singing and dancing that must have been taking place as the community gathered. "And the food!" he thought as he took another bite of the bland pita he would be calling lunch today. Perhaps that's what he missed most when he was left in the fields. In his mind's eye he could see his older brothers enjoying the fresh roasted lamb that was surely on the menu.

David knew that loneliness was part of the life of a shepherd, a life that was destined to be his. His father owned large flocks, and in Bethlehem, sons always followed in their father's footsteps. Yes, it was true that three of David's older brothers had left home to join King Saul's army, and at times David himself dreamed of fighting great battles for God and Israel. But then reality always set in. He was the last of Jesse's eight sons, and by the time he was old enough to be a soldier, all seven of his older brothers would surely have already enlisted. There was no way his father would let his youngest son enlist. Who would care for the flock? As he looked over the sheep grazing in the pasture around him, David knew that this was his future.

There were times when he thought of solitude as his friend. It was certainly better than some of the family times he had endured. It was true his father was highly regarded in the community, and anyone in Bethlehem would tell you that David came from a good family. But David almost laughed when he thought of that: "a good family," not with the way his brothers picked on him. He had sisters old enough to be his mother. Sometimes he felt he had more in common with his nephews than his own brothers and sisters. He thought highly of his father, but deep down inside he wished his father thought more highly of him. Jesse was so proud of his soldier sons; he would do anything for them. Yet here he was watching sheep while the rest of the family were the guests of the prophet at the community festival. Would it have been too much trouble to send one of the servants to watch the sheep so David could have been part of the feast?

As David looked at a young lamb struggling to keep up with the others, he thought, "That's the way I feel sometimes, like the runt of the litter." Gently, he lifted the awkward lamb and carried it to a patch of tender grass. As he set it down and watched it begin grazing contently, a smile came to David's face. "Alone," he thought, then concluded, "No. I am never really alone," as he looked into the clear blue sky. He sat on a large flat rock on the hillside and began singing a song he had written in the fields surrounding Bethlehem. He had written several songs, but already this one was becoming his favorite. Could he ever have imagined how many listeners would enjoy this song above all the others he would write?

"The LORD is my shepherd; I shall not want. He makes me to lie down in green pastures; He leads me beside the still waters. He restores my soul; He leads me in the paths of righteousness for His name's sake" (Psalm 23:1-3). David concluded that, if he was destined to be a shepherd, it would not be so bad after all. In fact, God had been a shepherd to him throughout his life. As he thought back on some of the more difficult times he had experienced, his meditation on God's work in his life turned to a song of praise directed to God Himself.

"Yea, though I walk through the valley of the shadow of death, I will fear no evil; for You are with me; Your rod and Your staff, they comfort me" (Psalm 23:4). David thought of some of the deep valleys through which he had led his flock as they moved from pasture to pasture. He had noticed how unsettled the sheep had been as they passed through the long shadows cast by the setting sun. Although he was still young, he realized there had been times when he had sensed that same fear in his own life. As he glanced over his flock again to be sure there were no predators on the horizon, he recalled the sensation of sheer terror that hit the moment he caught sight of a bear or lion within striking distance of his flock. But just as his presence had a calming influence on his sheep in the valley, so the awareness of God's presence had brought tranquility to his soul, enabling him to rise to the challenge of protecting the flock.

The noise of the celebration in the village still echoed across the valley, but by now David had other things on his mind. He might be missing out on an opportunity to dine with Israel's beloved prophet Samuel, but what did that really matter? "You prepare a table before me in the presence of my enemies," he sang, "You anoint my head with oil; my cup runs over" (Psalm 23:5). He was exactly where he wanted to be, enjoying the presence of God. And deep down he knew the best was yet to come. "Surely goodness and mercy shall follow me all the days of my life; and I will dwell in the house of the LORD forever" (Psalm 23:6).

GREAT LEADERS KNOW THEY ARE NEVER TRULY ALONE

A SEASON TO GROW

A generation later, David's son, Solomon, would write, "To

everything there is a season, a time for every purpose under heaven" (Ecclesiastes 3:1). Perhaps David understood that his responsibility as a shepherd placed him in an ideal setting for this season of growth in his life. He had ample opportunities to see and understand what so many others seemed to miss, living in the busy village. The long days and nights in the fields surrounding Bethlehem provided him time to think through the things he learned, enabling him to reach conclusions that would guide him for a lifetime. He was establishing a pattern of growth in the early years of his life that would characterize the rest of his life.

David wrote psalms throughout his life. These beautiful Hebrew poems expressed his passion, frustration, enthusiasm, discouragement and joy. They provide us a window to his soul, revealing what was taking place inside as he passed through varied experiences. Many of these psalms were later incorporated into Israel's national hymnbook, which was used in the temple, homes, and synagogues to aid in the worship of God. Bible teachers generally agree that David probably wrote several of these psalms as he tended sheep in the fields of Bethlehem.

It is not hard to imagine David looking into the sky during a night watch and marveling at the wonder of the clear Palestinian night sky. "The heavens declare the glory of God; and the firmament shows His handiwork. Day unto day utters speech, and night unto night reveals knowledge. There is no speech nor language where their voice is not heard. Their line has gone out through all the earth and their words to the end of the world" (Psalm 19:1-4). "How could anyone look into the beauty of the night sky and not see the fingerprint of the Creator?" he may have mused.

The shepherds of Israel often looked to the night sky to discern information for their work. They did not engage in the superstition of astrology that consumed the minds of the pagan kings of nations surrounding Israel. Rather, they looked for signs of changing seasons. When certain constellations moved to a new place in the sky, they knew it was time to move from the valleys to mountain pastures. They would know it was time to move back to the valleys when the alignment of stars changed again. And they knew how both their sheep and the predators that threatened them would behave according to the waxing and waning of the moon.

But while others saw patterns of stars and the cycles of the moon, David saw beyond. The message of the night sky was bigger than the direction most shepherds gleaned. It shouted out how glorious the God who made it must be. This was so obvious to David that he must have wondered about those who failed to hear the joyful chorus all nature seemed to sing. Perhaps those who rested in their own beds back in the village during the night watches could be excused, but David heard the same chorus as the sun traveled its path across the sky during daylight hours. "In them He has set a tabernacle for the sun, which is like a bridegroom coming out of his chamber, and rejoices like a strong man to run its race. Its rising is from one end of heaven, and its circuit to the other end; and there is nothing hidden from its heat" (Psalm 19:4-6).

GREAT LEADERS SEE AND UNDERSTAND WHAT OTHERS OVERLOOK

David was not only a student of the sky; he was also a student of the Scriptures. In both, he saw God revealing Himself to His people. Even though he might never be more than a shepherd, his father had taught him to read. Of course there was not much to read in the village of Bethlehem, but somehow David had managed to secure a copy of the Scriptures, and as he read those pages he realized he was reading a book destined to change lives.

Years later, the historians of Israel would record the work of Elijah and the school of the prophets, but leave few clues as to the origin of that school. Many Bible teachers believe the school may have begun under the ministry of Samuel, and that David may have been among his students. Much of Samuel's ministry was itinerate in nature, traveling along a regular circuit teaching the people the things of God. Perhaps that is where David first held the pages of the sacred text.

The law of God was given to Israel through Moses, a law that spoke to various aspects of society in the chosen nation. It was inevitable that kings would someday rule this people God had redeemed from slavery, so part of that law defined both the responsibilities and restrictions of that office. "Also it shall be, when he sits upon the throne of his kingdom, that he shall write for himself a copy of this law in a book, from the one before the priests, the Levites. And it shall be with him, and he shall read it all the days of his life, that he may learn to fear the LORD his God and be careful to observe all the words of this law and these statutes, that his heart may not be lifted up above his brethren, that he may not turn aside from the commandment to the right hand or to the left, and that he may prolong his days in his kingdom, he and his children in the midst of Israel" (Deuteronomy 17:18-20).

The law of God required that the king appointed by God should be a student of that law. David and much of Israel must have realized that Saul would have been a better king had he followed this condition. And if the daily study of the law could make a king a better king, then perhaps the same discipline would make a shepherd a better shepherd. It is not inconceivable to imagine David copying long sections of the law as he listened to Samuel teaching it. David certainly knew the law well, and knew the impact it had when applied to his own life.

"The law of the LORD is perfect, converting the soul; the testimony of the LORD is sure, making wise the simple; the statutes of the LORD are right, rejoicing the heart; the commandment of the LORD is pure, enlightening the eyes; the fear of the LORD is clean, enduring forever; the judgments of the LORD are true and righteous altogether" (Psalm 19:7-9). All this and more had been true in David's life. "More to be desired are they than gold, yea, than much find gold; sweeter also than honey and the honeycomb" (Psalm 19:10). David was convinced that his own experience with the Scriptures would be duplicated in the life of anyone who would consistently study and apply them. "Moreover by them Your servant is warned, and in keeping them there is great reward" (Psalm 19:11).

GREAT LEADERS READ GREAT BOOKS AND LET THEM SHAPE THEIR VALUES

All that David saw in the skies and the Scriptures pointed to God enthroned in majesty. How could he not shout out praises to his God? "O LORD, our Lord, how excellent is Your name in all the earth" (Psalm 8:1, 9). His glory far exceeded that which David had seen in the heavens as he gazed into the night sky. It seemed there could be no words sufficient to express the majesty of his God. Indeed, throughout much of his life he would struggle to use words to describe even a part of the majesty he beheld. Already God was his Shepherd (Psalm 23:1), his Strength, and his Savior (Psalm 19:14), but He would become much more in the years to come. Perhaps David knew that he would never succeed in adequately and completely describing the greatness of his God, but he would continue to try.

A. W. Tozer once wrote, "Without doubt, the mightiest thought the mind can entertain is the thought of God, and the weightiest word in any language is its word for God."[1] He added, "Perverted notions about God soon rot the religion in which they appear. The long career of Israel demonstrates this clearly enough, and the history of the Church confirms it. So necessary to the Church is a lofty concept of God that when that concept in any measure declines, the Church with her worship and her moral standards declines along with it. The first step down for any church is taken when it surrenders its high opinion of God."[2] David's thoughts of God were certainly high. He had an insight into the character and majesty of God that was indeed rare in his day.

In David's mind, people can't think great thoughts about God without changing the way they think about themselves. "When I consider Your heavens, the work of Your fingers, the moon and the stars, which You have ordained, what is man that you are mindful of him, and the son of man that You visit him" (Psalm 8:3, 4)? How can a mere mortal contemplate God without being a little overwhelmed? In the presence of God, people should begin to see themselves differently than before. Things that were once hidden are exposed and that which was previously acceptable now falls far short.

In the anguish of the moment, David must have cried out to God. "Who can understand his errors? Cleanse me from my secret faults. Keep back Your servant also from presumptuous sins; let them not have dominion over me. Then I shall be blameless, and I shall be innocent of great transgression" (Psalm 19:12, 13). As he prayed humbly before his God, David's worship carried a more subdued tone. "Let the words of my mouth and the meditation of my heart be acceptable in Your sight, O LORD, my strength and my Redeemer" (Psalm 19:14).

GREAT LEADERS HUMBLE THEMSELVES BEFORE A GREATER GOD

Given the dynamics evident in David's family, one might expect him to have a somewhat morose and negative perception of himself. But David's experience with God allowed him to understand the great worth that God as Creator had bestowed on him. True, in the context of contemplating the majesty of God, David could do little else but humble himself before God and acknowledge that there was indeed much in his life about which he should be humble. Yet David understood that God, as great as He was, had taken a personal interest in His people.

"For You have made him a little lower than the angels, and You have crowned him with glory and honor. You have made him to have dominion over the works of Your hands; You have put all things under his feet, all sheep and oxen – even the beasts of the field, the birds of the air, and the fish of the sea that pass through the paths of the seas" (Psalm 8:6-8). The people in whom God Himself had taken such an interest should hardly mope in misery. Even if they struggled to find value within themselves, they could be confident that God valued them greatly.

Could it be that God had a bigger plan for David than shepherding sheep for the rest of his life? It must have been almost too much for David to comprehend. It was certainly not something he could discuss with his family. To his father, he would always be his youngest boy, never quite able to measure up to his older brothers who were already his father's pride and joy. Certainly his own brothers were unlikely to entertain thoughts of David's success. He could almost hear the eldest, Eliab, laugh as he considered the idea himself. We can imagine there were many times when he felt like he was part of a family to which he never really belonged. But maybe, just maybe, God had something significant for him too.

GREAT LEADERS HAVE A BALANCED PERSPECTIVE OF WHO THEY TRULY ARE AND COULD BECOME

A NEGLECTED SON

David was surely not surprised if members of his own family overlooked him. As the eighth son of Jesse, he must have come to accept life as the low man on the totem pole. If honor was to come to the sons of Jesse, there were seven recipients standing in line before anyone would ever think of him. In Israel, birth order was everything; Eliab, the firstborn, would bear the family honor and the fate of Jesse's other sons was sealed. Even Abinadab could have only hoped that something would happen to Eliab before Jesse passed on his blessing to his sons, but that was not very likely. In David's case, seven older brothers would have had to die before he could ever hope to be the honored son.

Being the runt of the litter also meant David spent most of his time looking up to others in the family. In the last year or so, physical changes taking place in David's body had surely gone unnoticed in a family of much taller and stronger sons. Perhaps someday David would be as tall and strong as the others. Even with the more rapid growth he was experiencing in his teen years, he was just then approaching the height of his mother and older sisters.

His family was surely no different, in some respects, from others in the village, tending to make judgments upon what they could see without investigating things further. When they saw the sons of Jesse, they saw three soldiers in the army of Saul. They were not likely to see David's heart of courage that had fought a lion and bear to protect his father's sheep. It seemed unlikely that few would ever see the strength in David. It is not hard to imagine that when he first reported the tales of his struggles to his older brothers, they let him know that they thought it was a good story but could see right through it. "Really now! Little David taking on a bear and lion; and winning?" The laughter would echo in David's ears. It would be a long time before he would tell anyone else what happened.

Perhaps David's family's attitude got to him. Were there moments of anger? Was their treatment of him wrong but there was nothing he could do to change it? He may have felt about to drown in a pool of pity as, in the sibling dynamics of this family, he could easily have felt that he was on the outside looking in.

But such moments of lapse would be tempered by David's understanding of the ways God had worked in the past. It seemed like God specialized in taking small things and making something great out of them. He had taken an old man, Abraham, a worshipper of the moon god, and made his people a great nation devoted to Jehovah. He had taken a jailed slave in Egypt, Joseph, and made him the savior of his people. He had taken a nation of slaves and brought them into a land that flowed with milk and honey. He had taken an ox goad in the hand of Shamgar and the jawbone of a donkey in the hand of Samson to deliver Israel from the Philistines. Had he not chosen Israel's king from the smallest of Israel's tribes? Perhaps God could do something with "little David" after all.

It would be several centuries before a New Testament apostle would express the principle upon which David surely clung to. "For you see your calling, brethren, that not many wise according to the flesh, not many mighty, not many noble, are called. But God has chosen the foolish things of the world to put to shame the wise, and God has chosen the weak things of the world to put to shame the things which are mighty; and the base things of the world and the things which are despised God has chosen, and the things which are not, to bring to nothing the things which are, that no flesh should glory in His presence" (1 Corinthians 1:26-29).

GREAT LEADERS RISE ABOVE THE CONDITIONS INTO WHICH THEY WERE BORN

A REJECTED KING

Perhaps David's family experiences gave him a bit of a soft spot for King Saul. He had heard the rumors. By now all Israel had heard. The relationship between Israel's prophet and king had obviously deteriorated. Their most recent meetings had been marked by hostile exchanges. At their last meeting, Samuel had told the king, "The LORD has torn the kingdom of Israel from you today, and has given it to a neighbor of yours, who is better than you" (1 Samuel 15:28). The neglected son must have found it easy to identify with the pain of a rejected king.

It had not always been that way. Samuel was the one God appointed to anoint Saul as Israel's first king. It was doubtful anyone else in Israel had gained enough widespread support and respect for such a task. Previously, from the time of Moses, Israel had been ruled by judges. Some had reigned better than others. Most of the people seemed to agree that Samuel was among the best. For a time, it had been assumed that Samuel's sons, Joel and Abijah, would carry on as judges. But not long after they began serving with their father, it became apparent that they did not possess their father's godly character.

Joel and Abijah "did not walk in his ways; they turned aside after dishonest gain, to bribes, and perverted justice" (1 Samuel 8:3). Their behavior was more than the people of Israel were prepared to take. Before long, a delegation of elders arranged a meeting with Samuel, but their purpose was not to simply discuss the situation. They had already decided upon what they wanted and arrived prepared to give Samuel their demand. "Now make us a king to judge us like all the nations" (1 Samuel 8:5).

Initially, Samuel tried to discourage them by painting a bleak picture of what a king might do, but the people stood firm in their resolve. The idea of a king enslaving them and taxing them seemed too fantastic. It is possible that some viewed Samuel's warning as the desperate attempt of an old man trying to save his sons' jobs. They wanted a king and would continue making their demand until they got one. Eventually, Samuel was instructed by God to find them a king.

Samuel's choice was Saul, the son of Kish. He was everything the people wanted in a king – tall, dark and handsome, standing head and shoulders above those who had gathered for the announcement. Enthusiasm for Samuel's choice was evident throughout the crowd. "Long live the king!" they chanted so loudly that it must have been heard in neighboring villages (1 Samuel 10:24). The heads of each of Israel's families eagerly presented gifts to honor their new king. No doubt many who offered gifts that day hoped it might win them favor, should the time come when they needed the favor of the king.

There were of course some who were reluctant to accept the new king. This was to be expected. "How can this man save us?"

they questioned (1 Samuel 10:27). They could not conceive of any condition in which they might require the favor of this king, so they chose not to waste their money on a gift. Their actions did not go unnoticed, but Saul "held his peace" (1 Samuel 10:27). It was a day of celebration, not a time to begin disputes.

Saul quickly proved that he had what it took to be king. In his victory over the Ammonites and rescue of Jabesh Gilead, the people of Israel rallied to their new king's side. Some wanted to use the occasion to rid Israel of the critics once and for all, but Saul refused. "Not a man shall be put to death this day, for today the LORD has accomplished salvation in Israel" (1 Samuel 11:13). Samuel used the occasion of the victory to conduct a coronation and formally inducted Saul into his regal office.

Things had begun well in the reign of Saul, but eventually another side of the king began to emerge. In his frustration over waiting for Samuel to offer a sacrifice before going to war with the Philistines, Saul intruded into the priest's office and offered it himself, finishing just as Samuel arrived. The scene turned nasty with Samuel telling Saul, "But now your kingdom shall not continue. The LORD has sought for Himself a man after His own heart, and the LORD has commanded him to be commander over His people, because you have not kept what the LORD commanded you" (1 Samuel 13:14). It was a long time before the two men talked again.

Just when it seemed like Samuel and Saul had reconciled their differences, things went from bad to worse. It was hard to imagine how the rift between the two men could ever be repaired. Samuel sent Saul out to battle against the people of Amalek, assuring him of God's blessing and the promise of victory. Saul was told to destroy everything associated with the longstanding enemy of Israel, but Saul only did part of the job, saving the king to be his personal slave and livestock for the sacrificial altar. The dispute that followed was widely known throughout Israel. This was the last time the two men had met. Barring a miracle, it would be the last time the two men would ever meet.

Perhaps Saul's situation was ordained from the beginning. David had good reason to wonder why God had directed Samuel to anoint a man from the tribe of Benjamin to be Israel's king. Certainly Samuel was aware of the prophecy of the patriarch Jacob. "The scepter shall not depart from Judah, nor a lawgiver from beneath his feet, until Shiloh comes; and to Him shall be the obedience of the people" (Genesis 49:10). By that standard alone it would seem that David's own father would make a better king than Saul, as he had been born into the right tribe.

GREAT LEADERS LEARN FROM THE FAILURES OF OTHERS

A SELECTED KING

With the relationship between Israel's prophet and king deteriorating, there must have been tension in the air when one of the two arrived in any city. We can imagine that the people did not want to take sides in the dispute. If one appeared loyal to the prophet, they ran the risk of falling victim to the wrath of the king. On the other hand, if one was too loyal to the king, might not the prophet pray down the wrath of God upon their village? When the elders of Bethlehem saw Samuel coming up the road to their town, they were surely gripped with fear.

"Do you come peaceably?" they asked (1 Samuel 16:4). Samuel assured the elders he had a religious purpose in mind. "I have come to sacrifice to the LORD," he assured them (1 Samuel 15:5), which was only half the truth. He had heard from God and was about to reveal Israel's new king. The sacrifice was a ruse. It was intended to fool Saul and protect both Samuel and the one about to be anointed king. All he knew when he arrived in Bethlehem was that the king would be one of the sons of Jesse. As Jesse was a leading elder in Israel, it was only natural that he and his sons would join the celebration involved with the offering of a sacrifice.

There was a part of Samuel that understood this mission might be the riskiest of his long career. If Saul found out – he did not want to even think of that possibility. He knew what he had to do, and he wanted to do it quickly. He could make it look natural. No one would suspect anything if the prophet simply asked Jesse to present his sons and he were to anoint one at random. Of course, there would be nothing random about it. He would anoint the son who would be king, as soon as God told him which son that might be.

Samuel breathed a deep sigh of relief as he saw Jesse bringing his oldest son, Eliab, toward him. Obviously, this was the one, he concluded. He was the firstborn, the one most worthy of the honor this would bring to the family. Look at him – he just looked like a king. But as Samuel tightened his grip on the anointing oil he had brought with him for this occasion, he began hearing that still small voice and was stopped in his tracks. "Do not look at his appearance or at his physical stature, because I have refused him. For the LORD does not see as man sees; for man looks at the outward appearance, but the LORD looks at the heart" (1 Samuel 16:7).

Apart from God's direction it would be easy to make a mistake. Samuel recalled that Saul too once looked like a king. Politely he greeted Eliab and waited for Jesse to bring forward his next son. But Abinadab was not the one God had chosen either. Nor was it Shammah who was to be anointed king. They might be mighty warriors in the army of Saul, but neither was the king God had chosen. Four more sons passed before Samuel, but he was sure Israel's next king was not among them either. Could he have taken such a great risk and been wrong after all? "Are all the young men here?" Samuel asked his host. When he learned of David, he urged, "Send and bring him. For we will not sit down till he comes here" (1 Samuel 16:11).

David must have been surprised when one of his father's servants arrived to replace him and sent him back to the feast. To think, the whole feast would be delayed until he arrived. That certainly was different! Tempted as he was to walk and make those who had neglected him wait a little longer, he raced home to discover what this could mean. As he arrived and looked around the room, he thought he saw Samuel's eyes light up as the prophet glanced at him. He had not taken time to clean himself up as his brothers had. He still had the smell of the field on his clothes and he could only imagine how windblown his hair must have looked. For a moment, he was embarrassed at being the center of attention. He was not used to this!

"Then Samuel took the horn of oil and anointed him in the midst of his brothers" (1 Samuel 16:13). In his account of this event, the Jewish historian Josephus adds, "and whispered him in the ear, and acquainted him that God chose him to be their king; and exhorted him to be righteous, and obedient to his commands, for that by this means his kingdom would continue for a long time, and that his house should be of great splendor, and celebrated in the world; that he should overthrow the Philistines; and that against what nations soever he should make war, he should be the conqueror, and survive the fight; and that while he lived he should enjoy a glorious name, and leave such a name to his posterity also."[3]

GREAT LEADERS EMERGE FOR A GREAT PURPOSE

THE HEART OF A KING

Though still a young man, some things had already begun to emerge in David's life that suggested he might someday rise above his peers. Already he had experienced some success in the work for which he was responsible. His vigilance in keeping watch over his father's flock had resulted in the death of at least one bear and a lion (1 Samuel 17:36). Perhaps there were also wild dogs whose lives had been ended by a stone from the sling of David. In another age, Jesus would teach His disciples, "He who is faithful in what is least is faithful also in much; and he who is unjust in what is least is unjust also in much" (Luke 16:10).

But David was more than just a shepherd. He was also a skilled harpist, easily one of the best in the nation. It was the one area of his life where people actually recognized him for what he had accomplished. Though still young, many had heard him play. Those who heard him often told others, who also wanted to hear him play. His reputation had grown to the point where it was known even in the king's palace. Samuel may have just anointed him king over Israel, but it was his skill on the harp that would soon result in an invitation to Saul's palace.

While others might strive to find evidence of leadership in the early life of David, God had a different perspective. He looked beyond the visible and read the character etched on his heart. And when God looked on the heart of David, he saw dependability. Though only a young shepherd, David had assumed responsibility for his father's flock and acted accordingly (1 Samuel 17:34). As He looked further, God also saw courage. It was courage that overcame the moment of terror that gripped every shepherd when he came face to face with a predator (1 Samuel 17:35). "The wicked flee when no one pursues, but the righteous are bold as a lion" (Proverbs 28:1). God saw that David's heart was marked with characteristics that issued forth in action. He had been proactive in attacking those who would dare attack the flock (1 Samuel 17:36). And God saw in David a heart that would always honor God. Despite his efforts in protecting the flock, David was eager to give God the credit for his deliverance (1 Samuel 17:37). "In all your ways acknowledge Him, and He shall direct your paths" (Proverbs 3:6).

David's character could have only been deepened during the long days and lonely nights he spent in the field of Bethlehem. Helen Keller noted, "Character cannot be developed in ease and quiet. Only through experience of trial and suffering can the soul be strengthened, ambition inspired, and success achieved." The process, which had begun in the heart of the young shepherd, would continue many years before that shepherd would rule as sovereign over all Israel.

GREAT LEADERS
GROW FROM WITHIN

A NEW BEGINNING

As the oil from Samuel's horn dripped down David's head and onto his clothes, something else began to occur in the young shepherd's life. He had experienced a similar sensation only rarely, usually as he wrote one of his songs. But this time, it was different. There was a greater intensity than he had felt on previous occasions. "And the Spirit of the LORD came upon David from that day forward" (1 Samuel 16:13).

The act of anointing was the means by which prophets, priests and kings were inducted into office. These offices were so significant in the life of Israel that the people recognized the full duties of the office could not be completed without the aid of God. They became known as "the anointed offices" because those who held them would subject themselves to an anointing with oil which outwardly showed their dependence upon God to fulfill their tasks. When a prophet or priest anointed someone to one of these offices, it was also a statement that God intended to use that person in His special service.

Each of the anointed offices pointed ahead to their fulfillment in Jesus. The Hebrew title "Messiah" and Greek title "Christ" both mean "anointed one." Of Him it is said, "Therefore God, Your God, has anointed You with the oil of gladness more than Your companions" (Psalm 45:7; Hebrews 1:9). Jesus Himself acknowledged this anointing when He applied the prophecy of Isaiah to Himself. "The Spirit of the Lord GOD is upon Me, because the LORD has anointed Me to preach good tidings to the poor" (Isaiah 61:1; Luke 4:18).

The anointing oil held its own special significance in this ritual of ancient Israel. It was one of several Old Testament emblems of the Holy Spirit. When a man passed through the anointing ritual, it was a testimony of an even greater reality. He who was anointed with oil recognized his need to be anointed by the Spirit of God for power to accomplish the task he was about to undertake.

"This blessed anointing for service cannot be ours unless there has been a previous gracious work on the heart," explains F. B. Meyer. "There must be the new life – the life of God. There must be docility, humility, fidelity to duty, cleansing from known sin, and a close walk with God. The descending flame must fall upon the whole burnt-offering of a consecrated life. And it was because all these had been accomplished in David by the previous work of the Holy Spirit that he was prepared for this special unction."[4]

Some might view this special blessing from God as the climax of their spiritual life. David understood that it was the beginning. God had chosen him to serve a unique role in the life of his nation. He, and others in Israel like him, no doubt had begun to see evidence that they were a nation in decline. If everything rises and falls on leadership, then the task to which he was being called was critical. God had a work for David, and though just a young shepherd, he understood it would be foolish to undertake the work of God without the power of God. As the oil dripped slowly down his head and face, he knew the adventure had just begun.

GREAT LEADERS SERVE BY THE POWER OF THE SPIRIT OF GOD

CHAPTER TWO

WHEN THE ENEMY THREATENS TO EAT YOU ALIVE

1 Samuel 16:14-17:58

As David adjusted to his new experience with God, another man in the kingdom was making an even greater adjustment.

As Israel's first king, Saul also knew what it felt like to experience a special endowment of power from God to perform the task to which he was called. Like David, Saul's experience with the Spirit of God had been linked to Samuel and a special anointing. In a private meeting while Israel was first demanding a king, "Samuel took a flask of oil and poured it on his head" (1 Samuel 10:1). Saul was made aware of the significance of this act and given specific instructions by the prophet.

Saul's initial encounter with Samuel was not planned; at least not by the one who would become Israel's first king. He had left home at his father's request looking for donkeys that had wandered from his father's herd. Together with a trusted servant, he searched through various regions without success. When Saul finally concluded that it was time to return home before his father worried about him, his servant suggested visiting the prophet living in Ramah. Since the city was nearby, Saul reluctantly agreed, assuming Samuel might be able to discern the location of his father's donkeys. God, however, had already prepared Samuel for a larger task.

The day before his encounter with Saul, Samuel had heard directly from God. He had whispered in the prophet's ear to alert him of the significance of the apparently chance meeting about to take place. "Tomorrow about this time, I will send you a man from the land of Benjamin, and you shall anoint him commander over My people Israel, that he may save My people from the hand of the Philistines; for I have looked upon My people, because their cry has come to Me" (1 Samuel 9:15). When a man looking for donkeys arrived the next day, God reminded Samuel, "There he is, the man of whom I spoke to you. This one shall reign over My people" (1 Samuel 9:16).

Samuel was faithful to his calling in anointing Saul, yet there were things Saul needed to do himself. He was told to head toward Rachel's tomb, a well-known landmark in the territory of Benjamin. There he would be assured that his father's donkeys were indeed safe. He was instructed to then go to the Terebinth tree of Tabor and meet three men, and to accept their gifts. Then Saul was to head to Bethel, "the hill of God," even though there was currently a Philistine garrison stationed there. Samuel added, "Then the Spirit of the LORD will come upon you, and you will prophesy with them and be turned into another man" (1 Samuel 10:6).

Saul immediately did as he was instructed, and everything Samuel predicted did happen. "When he came there to the hill, there was a group of prophets to meet him; then the Spirit of God came upon him, and he prophesied among them" (1 Samuel 10:10). Although such an experience with God was rare through-out the Old Testament and highly valued by those to whom it was given, Saul quickly became embarrassed by the occurrence.

Those who knew Saul best certainly knew that the lifestyle he lived was distinct from that expected of a prophet. Also, his fami-ly's business involved raising donkeys, an animal considered unclean under Israel's kosher food laws. This hardly made Saul a candidate for prophet in Israel. When Saul's friends heard his story, they laughed in disbelief and exclaimed, "What is this that has come upon the son of Kish? Is Saul also among the prophets?"

(1 Samuel 10:11). Saul was so embarrassed at their response that he decided to tell no one else what had taken place. Even when his uncle learned of his visit with Samuel and directly asked him what Samuel had said, Saul remained silent "about the matter of the kingdom" (1 Samuel 10:16).

Although his first experience with the Spirit of God had been embarrassing to him, Saul did recognize that God's spirit brought him success in his first battle. When he learned of the plight of Jabesh Gilead, "the Spirit of God came upon Saul...and his anger was greatly aroused" (1 Samuel 11:6). In the passion of the moment, he was able to channel that anger to raise an army and gain a significant victory over the Ammonites. Even though his personal walk with God did not seem to be as strong as it should have been, Saul apparently valued the presence of God, if for no other reason than it guaranteed victory in battle.

"But the Spirit of the LORD departed from Saul" (1 Samuel 16:14). As David sought to adjust to the reality of God's presence in his life, Saul began adjusting to His absence. One would be hard pressed to find a more difficult task in life. According to F. B. Meyer, "Nothing in this world or the next can be compared for horror to the withdrawal of God from us. It involves the perdition of body and soul, because it is the one force by which evil is restrained and good fostered. Take the sun from the center of the solar system, and each planet, breaking from its leash, would pursue a headlong course, colliding with the rest and dashing into the abyss. So when God's presence is lost, every power in the soul rises in revolt. Ah! bitter wail, when a man realizes the true measure of the calamity which has befallen him, and cries with Saul, "I am sore distressed; for God is departed from me, and answereth me no more."[1] In the midst of his own spiritual crisis years later, David would cry out to God, "Do not take Your Holy Spirit from me" (Psalm 51:11). When a Christian is walking in the flesh, they can not please God. (Romans 8:8) When a Christian is walking in the Spirit, they have God's power controlling their direction and actions. "If God be for us, who can be against us?" (Romans 8:31b).

GREAT LEADERS VALUE THEIR PERSONAL RELATIONSHIP WITH GOD

MUSIC CALMS THE SAVAGE BEAST

As difficult as it was for Saul to adjust to God's absence in his life, another condition served only to complicate the matter. "A distressing spirit from the LORD troubled him" (1 Samuel 16:14). The absence of the enabling Spirit of God made room for a disabling spirit to invade his life.

Jesus later warned His disciples of this very danger in the context of describing a man freed from the bondage of an evil spirit but not filled with the Holy Spirit. He taught, "When an unclean spirit goes out of a man, he goes through dry places, seeking rest, and finds none. Then he says, 'I will return to my house from which I came.' And when he comes, he finds it empty, swept, and put in order. Then he goes and takes with him seven other spirits more wicked than himself, and they enter and dwell there; and the last state of that man is worse than the first. So shall it be with this wicked generation" (Matthew 12:43-45). This became Saul's fate.

The spiritual bondage that now enslaved Saul may have been the result of his dabbling in the occult practices of the nations around Israel. Although such actions are not detailed in the biblical text, there are references that suggest Saul's heart had wandered from God long before his break with Samuel. He apparently named his forth son, Esh-Baal, in honor of Baal, the storm god widely worshipped in the region (1 Chronicles 8:33). Saul's first-born son, Jonathan, apparently followed the same practice in the naming of his first-born (1 Chronicles 8:33). Later, when Saul's daughter married David, she brought with her a household god (1 Samuel 19:13). Saul's growing involvement in idolatry and occult worship may have been recognized by Samuel, giving new insight into his warning to the wandering king. "For rebellion is as the sin of witchcraft, and stubbornness is as iniquity and idolatry. Because you have rejected the Word of the LORD, He also has rejected you from being king" (1 Samuel 15:23).

Saul's present condition added a whole new dimension to regular affairs of state. His extreme mood swings made him completely unpredictable and it became increasingly more difficult for his staff to serve him effectively. They would begin one project only to discover hours or days later that it no longer was of interest to their king. Actions taken one day might be reversed the next. A royal decree might be rescinded within weeks of its publication. Something had to be done, and quickly. The actions of the king impacted the whole nation.

Recognizing the seriousness of the situation, the palace staff ventured to discuss the issue with their king. The problem could no longer be hidden. Even Saul recognized that he was being plagued with a distressing spirit. The staff thought maybe music would help distract him from his melancholy mood, just as a song had often lifted their spirits. But they also knew they could not act independently on this matter. "Let our master now command your servants, who are before you, to seek out a man who is a skillful player on the harp," they pleaded. They could only hope the soothing music of the stringed instrument would have a calming influence. "And it shall be that he will play it with his hand when the distressing spirit from God is upon you, and you shall be well" (1 Samuel 16:16).

When Saul agreed to try their proposal, his staff faced another problem. Where would they find such an individual? Only recently had the nation of twelve tribes united under a single king. Other nations in the area had seen this uniting of the tribes as a threat to their security and had made it their business to make sure this effort did not succeed. Throughout much of Saul's reign, Israel was a nation at war with its neighbors, fighting for its own survival. The struggle had touched every family in the land. Where would they find a musician in a nation of soldiers?

What they needed was not just any musician, but one whose passion for music had been developed through long hours of disciplined practice. One might learn three chords on a guitar and accompany songs around a campfire, but the musician they needed was being called on to play for a king. They could not take a chance on just anyone. The man they sought had to be a proven success already. His reputation for excellence must precede him.

David's long hours in Bethlehem pastures had provided him time that others in his trade often squandered. Others might have thought he was wasting time as he first began plucking away at the harp he carried. Before long, the irritating sound of missed notes and stretched strings gave way to recognizable tunes. Those who had previously tried to avoid "the noise" now gathered around and joined in the singing. Many who played the harp in Israel were content when their playing reached a level that brought acceptance from their peers, but David played for a greater audience. The songs he wrote were more than love songs and the ballads of great battle victories. He wrote songs and played his harp to celebrate the majesty of God Himself. The theme of his song motivated him to develop his skill beyond the expectations of others. He had to play the best he possibly could if he would play for God.

GREAT LEADERS PURSUE EXCELLENCE IN EVERYTHING THEY DO

David's disciplined pursuit of excellence had not gone unnoticed. His reputation had spread far beyond his village as travelers through Bethlehem told others of the beautiful music they heard from the harp of the young boy. A member of Saul's own staff had been to Bethlehem and heard David's playing for himself. "Look," he explained to his peers as they wondered how they would implement their plan. "I have seen a son of Jesse the Bethlehemite, who is skillful in playing" (1 Samuel 16:18). He was convinced David could be the solution to their problem. They could bring him to

Gibeah as "a mighty man of valor, a man of war" and continue hiding the king's situation from the general public. He was sure that David would be "prudent in speech" and not spread rumors about their king. The servant remembered David was "a handsome person" and he would not be an embarrassment to those focused on the image of the palace (1 Samuel 16:18).

There was something else he remembered about David. The palace staff had not spoken of it with Saul, but they knew the evil spirit was only part of the problem. The Spirit of God was now gone. This Spirit had so empowered their king previously that people wanted to follow him. Even those who did not know the reason knew that something that used to be there was no longer present. Maybe David could help with that problem too. "The LORD is with him," the servant explained (1 Samuel 16:18).

The matter was quickly settled. David seemed to be the answer to everyone's concerns. He had extraordinary talent and would fit their chosen cover story for bringing him to the royal city. Once there, he could be counted on to hold his tongue and would look like he belonged in the palace. And for those who believed Saul's problem was deeper, David's arrival could mark the return of the Spirit of God to the city. Counting on Jesse's loyalty to their king, they asked him to send his son to Gibeah without explanation. As expected, Jesse obeyed the royal summons.

When David arrived, he was presented to the king and immediately made a positive first impression. There was something about David that Saul found appealing. Even if he could not play the harp, David was the kind of man Saul wanted near him. The king established a plausible cover story for the real reason David had been summoned – David was appointed as his armor-bearer and a more formal request was issued from the throne to Jesse. When kings make requests, citizens know better than to refuse. The ruse was complete and David had a valid reason for being in the royal city.

Only a few knew the real reason David was there. Initially, even David was not aware of the king's struggle, but before long, he was apprised of the situation. Israel had many soldiers, but there were none who could play with the skill of David. David may have been disappointed to learn that a promising military career was in reality a series of musical concerts that could never be discussed with others. Regardless of his personal feelings, he came to perceive his musical gifts as a means of serving his king, and ultimately the nation. "And so it was, whenever the spirit from God was upon Saul, that David would take a harp and play it with his hand. Then Saul would become refreshed and well, and the distressing spirit would depart from him" (1 Samuel 16:23).

Even as a young musician, David most likely realized that music held a power not often understood by non-musicians. The emotional power of music has long been widely recognized, as music can change the way one feels. It has the ability to bring tears to the eyes or a smile to the face. When David played his harp, Saul's mood was refreshed.

Few people understand that music can also physically affect people. A driving base rhythm in a song can have a negative effect on those with cardiac problems. In contrast, soothing music can aid in the healing of those whose illness is aggravated by stress. When David played his harp, Saul's body became well.

Music can also have a spiritual impact on people. Many religions encourage their disciples to chant or sing to their gods. In light of the biblical teaching concerning the origin of these religions, these songs can be the means of entering into spiritual bondage. In contrast, God inhabits the praises of His people (Psalm 22:3). Those who use music in the worship of God invite His presence into their life. When David played his harp, the distressing spirit departed.

As he played for his king, David saw confirmation of what he had heard from others on the royal staff. Although both physical and emotional problems could produce symptoms similar to those Saul was experiencing, Saul's problem was spiritual. He really needed the ministry of a prophet who would help him restore his fractured relationship with God, but the king had already rejected

Samuel's counsel. David did not have those spiritual endowments at this point in his life, but he could play the harp. He knew how music had helped him in his own walk with God. Throughout Israel, the harp was widely used as a source of entertainment. David would use it for a different purpose. Perhaps if he played well enough, his music could usher his king into the presence of his God. Maybe then, Saul's real problem could be dealt with and the nation would once more have a functioning monarch.

GREAT LEADERS USE PHYSICAL MEANS TO ACCOMPLISH SPIRITUAL GOALS

FROM THE PALACE TO THE PASTURE

David's assignment at the palace had its desired effect, though not to the degree David might have hoped. Saul's staff was pleased with their king's recovery and the palace was once again able to function well. But no sooner had Saul's personal problem been dealt with than another crisis arose. Reports from Judah indicated that the nation would soon be at war.

While there were several nations near Israel that threatened the nation's security, none were as significant a threat as the Philistines. Their population was concentrated within an alliance of five city-states in the coastal plain, but their influence extended throughout Israel. Their superior weapons had given them an advantage in previous battles and in victory they had forcibly disarmed Israel. In order to ensure that the nation of Israel would not re-arm, the Philistines removed all blacksmiths, most likely enslaving them in the ironworks of Philistia (1 Samuel 13:19). Whenever an Israeli farmer needed to sharpen a plough or other tool of his trade, he had to journey into enemy territory and pay the customary service fee (1 Samuel 13:21). The plan accomplished its intended goal. "There was neither sword or spear found in the hand of any of the people who were with Saul and Jonathan. But they were found with Saul and Jonathan his son" (1 Samuel 13:22).

Jonathan's victory over the Philistines in a previous battle had improved the situation only slightly. A number of weapons had been recovered from fallen Philistine soldiers and those who had deserted in haste. A series of defensive victories over other invasion forces from neighboring enemies added to the arsenal. Still, only the Philistines had the blacksmiths who continually fashioned new weapons and sharpened their blades and points. A farmer might be able to get a plough sharpened in Philistia, but he was not likely to find a blacksmith that would sharpen his sword. No price would have been worth that risk.

Now the Philistines had begun mobilizing their troops once again. A large encampment had been spotted in Ephes Dammin, stretching between Sochoh and Azekah. It was clear they would march into the heart of Israel through the Valley of Elah and any attempt to stop them would occur there. Quickly, Saul issued the order and Israel's own army gathered once more under his leadership to battle their traditional enemies.

With all the focus on preparing for war, it may have been some time before the palace staff realized they had a problem of their own making. As Saul's armor-bearer, it would only be natural for David to accompany the king into battle. But the nature of a field camp would make it difficult to maintain the cover. Before long, soldiers who assembled for battle would realize that the King's armor-bearer was really not an armor-bearer at all. He practiced while others fought so he could play soothing songs for the king when he returned from battle. If they discovered the real reason David had been summoned to Gibeah, the effect on morale could be devastating. Once again, something had to be done.

David had done his job well in Gibeah; Saul's fits of rage and deep depression had become a distant memory to those who served closest to the king. The idea of removing David and his music may have seemed a risky thing to do, but those who had to make the decision felt that the risk was minimal compared to the greater risk that David's true purpose in the palace would be exposed. Even if the king began to lapse again, the adrenaline from daily conflicts with the Philistines should boost Saul's spirits. If David's services were needed again after the battle he would be brought back to Gibeah. But for now, he had to go.

It would be embarrassing for the king's armor-bearer to be dismissed from duty just when the battle was about to begin. Some who had grown fond of David tried to soften the blow. David's father was a respected elder in Bethlehem and he was not getting any younger. His three oldest sons were loyal soldiers in Saul's army. Knowing the difficulty that the absence of three sons would create in a family of shepherds, sending David home could appear to be a gesture of good will from the king as he gave up his own armor-bearer for the benefit of one of Judah's most respected families. David may not have been sure that the story would be widely accepted, but the decision had already been made. He was leaving the palace to return to the pastures of Bethlehem.

After a while, David had begun thinking Samuel's prophecy about him becoming king was right. He couldn't help but feel a little proud when he learned Saul had chosen him as his armor-bearer. That would give his father something to talk about in the city gate. Even when he learned the real reason he had been summoned to Gibeah, he could take comfort in the fact that no one outside the palace staff knew. Everyone still thought he was the king's armor-bearer. Soon, however, he would pass through the very gates in which his father had boasted, not as a soldier, but once again a shepherd. What made it worse was that he could not explain what was really going on. He had seen the improvement in Saul's mood as he prepared for battle in those few days before David left for home. Deep down he knew it would not be long before Saul would not even remember he existed.

For some, the circumstances David faced may have been too much to handle. While Saul and his army, including his brothers, went off to war to experience great adventure, David would again be left behind. As he walked through the pastures on the edge of Bethlehem tending his father's flocks, he must have imagined Eliab and his other brothers laughing around the campfire about the armor-bearer assigned to protect a few sheep in the wilderness. But David did not let the situation bother him anymore. He knew he was never really an armor-bearer, but he had served his king and country in a way no soldier could ever understand. Samuel had promised that someday he would be king, but right now that did not matter. If God had sent him back to his father's flocks, he would serve his father as faithfully as he had served his king.

GREAT LEADERS ARE MORE COMMITTED TO SERVICE THAN STATUS

A DEMORALIZED ARMY WAITING TO LOSE

While David tended his father's sheep, the battle lines were drawn on hills facing both sides of the Valley of Elah. Saul and his men began preparing themselves for the inevitable conflict about to take place. Even as they pitched tents and built campfires, they cautiously looked across the valley so as to not be caught off guard by a raiding party from the other side. Few in Israel would forget that such a party led by Jonathan had been the key to their greatest victory over the Philistines. Would the enemy now attempt a similar attack on Israel?

Their initial fear of a surprise attack would have been relieved when soldiers looked across the valley and saw smoke rising from the Philistine campfires. The enemy camp was so large they had no need for the element of surprise. The invasion force was a well-oiled military machine. Israel's army consisted of farmers and merchants who had set aside their commercial interests to engage in this time of military conflict. They fought with the passion of patriots, but neither their size nor skill could match that of the enemy. Still, it was their land and they would stand their ground to defend it. Most likely the battle would consist of a series of individual conflicts between soldiers from opposing sides, making victory possible for Israel. That was the way Israel's soldiers wanted to look at it.

Although sentries were posted in both camps during the night watches, soldiers on both sides knew there was little chance of a night battle. Fighting battles was hard enough when you could see what you were doing. Fighting a night battle was far too risky and would only occur as the act of a desperate army with little to lose. Neither side involved in this battle was that desperate, so the soldiers of both Israel and Philistia had a good night's sleep.

As the sun rose over the Judean hills, men on both sides rose and armed themselves for battle. Before long, David's brothers expected they would hear the sound of the shophar calling them to descend into the valley and fight. But the shophar would not sound this day. The Lords of the Philistines would propose another way to resolve this dispute. While foreign to Israel, their proposal was widely practiced by the Greeks and others who shared their polytheistic worldview.

Israel's worship of one God, termed monotheism, was a foreign concept to the other nations of the region. They also worshipped a god, but theirs was a regional deity and they were quite content to recognize the validity of the gods of other nations. In the fatalism that permeated the culture of that day, these nations believed everything was in the hands of the gods. They developed rituals and sacrificial systems designed to appease their god(s) so he or she would not turn on them. Sometimes these rituals were extreme to the point of offering human sacrifices. The gods had to be appeased at all costs.

No battle would begin without a sacrifice to the gods. These nations believed if their gods were pleased with them, they would fight on their behalf. In this respect, Israel had a similar view of the LORD of Hosts. Moses had taught Israel at the conclusion of a wilderness conflict to begin thinking of God as "Jehovah Nissi, The-LORD-Is-My-Banner" (Exodus 17:15). A long succession of military victories in the name of God only served to strengthen Israel's belief that their battles were God's battles (1 Samuel 17:47).

If the general fate of a nation was in the hands of its gods, then the fate of a nation in battle was in the hands of the strongest gods – this was the logical conclusion in a polytheistic world. Victories on the battlefield were perceived as a manifestation of the battles between the gods of the nations in conflict. This perspective helped people understand how sometimes small nations overcame incredible odds to win in conflict with larger and stronger nations. It also gave rise to a different way of looking at international conflict.

If the results on the battlefield were truly predetermined by a battle between rival gods in the heavens, then it was reasonable to look for a way to determine how the gods had fared rather than risk high casualties on the battlefield. The Greeks began adopting the practice of having a championship battle, with other nations following their example. Each side involved in a conflict would choose their champion soldier and agree to allow the two to fight to the death. The last one standing would indicate the victorious god in the heavenly conflict, represent the likely results of a fully armed conflict, and decide the conflict with fewer casualties.

As Israel's army looked across the valley for the advance of the Philistine army, to their surprise, two men made their way into the valley below. One was obviously the armor-bearer of the other. The other was enormous. He stood nine feet, nine inches tall and was made of solid muscle. He wore armor heavier than most men could think of lifting, yet seemed to be comfortable. When he spoke, his voice echoed clearly across the valley so every Israeli soldier could hear.

"Why have you come out to line up for battle?" he asked. "Am I not a Philistine, and you the servants of Saul? Choose a man for yourselves, and let him come down to me," he continued. "If he is able to fight with me and kill me, then we will be your servants. But if I prevail against him and kill him, then you shall be our servants and serve us." Then adding insult to injury, Goliath called out, "I defy the armies of Israel this day; give me a man, that we may fight together" (1 Samuel 17:8-10).

Martin Luther King, Jr. once said, "The ultimate measure of a man is not where he stands in moments of comfort, but where he stands at times of challenge and controversy." By this standard, Israel failed miserably. "When Saul and all Israel heard these words of the Philistine, they were dismayed and greatly afraid" (1 Samuel 17:11). Even the king who was taller than most men knew Goliath had the obvious advantage in one-on-one conflict. It was clear that anyone who ventured into such a battle would be engaged in a suicide mission.

For forty days the challenge was issued and never accepted. Some Bible teachers note the number forty is often used in Scripture to emphasize a time of evaluation. Even the promise of a tax-free life and marriage into the royal family would not likely motivate men to accept the challenge. Morale sank as the days passed. How could Israel ever find a champion to match Goliath's strength?

The soldiers in Saul's army were obviously not eager to send home information about what was taking place. About six weeks after sending his three oldest sons into the battle that never was, Jesse's concern for their welfare prompted him to take action. He gathered a wagon full of food and sent his youngest son to deliver the supplies and report back on the status of the battle.

David left early enough to arrive at the camp of Israel just as the army was preparing to engage the Philistines in battle. He quickly found the supply keeper and ran to find his brothers. He arrived just as Goliath made his daily appearance. And he stood and watched as the army of Israel retreated in terror. Everything he saw left him puzzled. As he began asking questions, others looked at him in disbelief. "Have you seen this man who has come up?" they asked (1 Samuel 17:25).

While others saw a giant that could not be conquered, David saw a man who had defied both God and the army of the people of God. He didn't see a giant, He saw God. His passion for God and patriotic zeal convinced him that such a man could not be allowed to continue his disrespect of the Almighty God David served. He found it difficult to believe no one had dealt with this problem yet. If no one else would do his duty and defend God's reputation and Israel's honor, then he would. "Let no one's heart fail because of him," David announced. "Your servant will go and fight with this Philistine" (1 Samuel 17:32). David did not see an opponent; he saw an opportunity for God to be glorified.

GREAT LEADERS RECOGNIZE CHALLENGING CIRCUMSTANCES AS SIGNIFICANT OPPORTUNITIES

IS THERE NOT A CAUSE?

David quickly learned of all that had been promised to the man who would defeat Goliath, but that had little to do with his motives. He simply could not fathom the idea that "this uncircumcised Philistine . . . should defy the armies of the living God" (1 Samuel 17:26). Making those kinds of statements did not make him popular among those who had watched Goliath daily for forty days. When word spread to Eliab about what his young brother was saying, his anger boiled over into harsh words. "Why did you come down here?" he snarled. "And with whom have you left those few sheep in the wilderness? I know your pride and the insolence of your heart, for you have come down to see the battle," he accused (1 Samuel 17:28).

David was unmoved by his brother's false accusations. "What have I done now?" he asked. "Is there not a cause?" (1 Samuel 17:29). The question silenced his brother and David began asking others the same thing. He must have known that he was the least qualified man on the hillside to face Goliath. Perhaps he hoped he could challenge others to rise to the occasion. If so, his efforts failed.

When word reached Saul that David was prepared to fight, the king knew this idea was ridiculous. How could a shepherd take on an experienced man of war and expect to win? But even his king's open expressions of doubt were insufficient to discourage David. It was true he was not a man of war, but he had fought his own battles on the hills surrounding Bethlehem. He reminded the king of his victory over lions and bears as he protected his father's flock. As far as he was concerned, Goliath was just one more predator that needed to be dealt with. He had "defied the armies of the living God" (1 Samuel 17:36).

Admittedly, Goliath was bigger than any lion or bear he had faced in the past, but that really didn't matter. He was well aware of his dependence upon God in facing those previous challenges. He would defeat Goliath the same way, by depending upon God. "The LORD, who delivered me from the paw of the lion and from the paw of the bear, He will deliver me from the hand of this Philistine," he announced (1 Samuel 17:37).

There was little Saul could do to stop him. David was determined to fight. He offered the young volunteer his armor, but their difference in size meant the armor was more of a hindrance than help. Saul figured David's declining the use of armor would make no difference in the expected outcome of the battle. David left the king's tent and made his way into the valley to meet the challenge. On the way, he stopped by a brook and picked up five stones that had been worn smooth by the water.

Goliath mocked and cursed David in the names of his Philistine gods as he saw the boy approaching. "Come to me, and I will give your flesh to the birds of the air and the beasts of the field," he cried out (1 Samuel 17:22). But David was not deterred by the mocking, curses or threats. He was fighting for a cause bigger than his personal ego. This was an opportunity to demonstrate to both the Philistines and Israelites that the God of Israel was indeed far greater than Dagon or any other Philistine deity.

"You come to me with a sword, with a spear, and with a javelin," David noted. "But I come to you in the name of the LORD of hosts, the God of the armies of Israel, who you have defied. This day the LORD will deliver you into my hand, and I will strike you and take your head from you. And this day I will give the carcasses of the camp of the Philistines to the birds of the air and the wild beasts of the earth, that all the earth may know

that there is a God in Israel. Then all this assembly shall know that
the LORD does not save with the sword and spear; for the battle
is the LORD's, and He will give you into our hands" (1 Samuel
17:45-47).

GREAT LEADERS PURSUE CAUSES WORTH PURSUING

JUST DAVID AND THE LORD OF HOSTS

The account of the battle in the Valley of Elah has become legendary. With a single stone from his slingshot, Goliath was defeated. As all who witnessed the event looked on in shock at the giant's
lifeless body, David took Goliath's own sword and decapitated his
enemy. As he lifted the giant's head high in victory, Israel's army
shouted in victory and advanced to do battle with a shocked and
demoralized Philistine army, which was already in retreat. Israel's
victory that day drove the Philistines back from their strongholds
and out of the territory of Judah.

In his book, *Search the Scriptures*, Dr. Robert B. Greenblatt
notes, "giants are prone to suffer from lateral blindness." He attributes David's victory over Goliath at least in part to Goliath's tunnel
vision. "His sight is clear in a direct line, but not peripherally.
David, therefore, would step agilely to the side when he had drawn
close enough to Goliath. Then, as his adversary hesitated, clumsi-
ly turning his head to bring back the youth within his limited field
of vision, David, undoubtedly skilled in the art of slinging, took
deadly aim with the slingshot and struck the lone spot unprotected by heavy armor. The blow on his forehead spelled defeat for the
giant. Thus David won his victory by superior knowledge, skill,
and agility, rather than by brute force."[2]

David attributed his success to an even greater source. As he
entered the valley that day, he was aware of three armies that had
gathered for battle. He could see the Philistine army in their camp

as he advanced toward Goliath. He was well aware of the army of Israel from whose camp he had just departed. And he was equally aware of the unseen army of heaven that had gathered on the battlefield that day. He was convinced that this army would gain the ultimate victory that day.

The Hebrew name Jehovah Tsabbaoth, translated "LORD of hosts," describes God as the ruler over the armies (hosts) of heaven and earth. There are at least two implications in this Old Testament name of God. First, it identifies Jehovah as the one who gives victory. Second, it suggests Jehovah will also give the power needed to achieve that victory. In Israel's early conquest of the Promised Land under Joshua, the concepts embodied in this name were widely recognized. Later, as Israel wandered from God, prophets and other leaders used this name of God to remind the nation of these principles.

When an ambassador speaks in the name of his or her country, all the power of that country is behind them, reinforcing what they say. When David spoke in the name of the LORD of hosts, he knew all the power of heaven's army was present to confirm his statement. Israel had forgotten what their God could do for them. As they looked across the valley, they saw a shepherd approaching an unbeatable giant. As David recognized the presence of the third army that day, he knew there was no way the giant would remain standing for long.

GREAT LEADERS TAKE ON GIANTS AGAINST WHOM THEY HAVE NO HOPE OF WINNING, AND WIN

FROM VICTORY TO VICTORY

While Israel fought the Philistines in the battle that followed Goliath's fall, David took the giant's head and went on his own personal mission.

There had been time to think as he pastured his father's sheep during much of this conflict with the Philistines. He was not sure how, but he was convinced Samuel's prophetic act would come to pass. All that he now knew about the secrets of Gibeah convinced him he would not choose to reign from that city. He would reign from Jerusalem, a city worthy of becoming a royal city. There was only one problem with this plan. Jerusalem had never been conquered in the four hundred years Israel had occupied the Promised Land. Most people thought of it as a city that could not be conquered.

As he came within sight of Jerusalem, we can imagine David sitting on a rock and looking at his gruesome trophy of war. "Israel thought you were invincible," he spoke boldly to the lifeless head. "But they were wrong. God gave you to me." Then, looking at the walls of the invincible city of Jerusalem, David announced, "And all Israel is wrong about you too. Someday, God will also give you to me." The battle for Jerusalem was years in the future, but David already knew how that battle would end.

GREAT LEADERS MAKE GREAT VICTORIES THE SPRINGBOARD FOR GREATER VICTORIES TO COME

CHAPTER THREE

WHEN THE BOSS LIKES
YOU BETTER DEAD

1 Samuel 18:1-19:24; Psalm 59:1-17

David's suspicions of Saul had been correct. Although his victory over Goliath took place less than two months after he left the palace in Gibeah, Saul did not remember him. But it was not just Saul who was suffering from memory loss. Saul's chief military officer also failed to remember him. Perhaps they could not be blamed. Now that they had begun winning battles against the Philistines again, no one wanted to remember those torturous days in the palace when it seemed like the kingdom itself might be in jeopardy.

Though he was not remembered, David did not go unnoticed. How could he? He was not old enough to qualify for military service under Israel's law, yet he had single-handedly defeated Goliath, an act that had reinvigorated Israel's army and marked the beginning of the victory being celebrated that day. When he was again in the presence of his king later that evening, he was still dragging the head of Goliath with him.

The meeting with Saul was brief. When asked to identify himself, he described himself as "the son of your servant Jesse the Bethlehemite" (1 Samuel 17:58). Even if Saul had forgotten David, it was unlikely he would have forgotten so prominent a leader in Judah as his father. But it was not Jesse who impressed Saul this day. It was not Jesse who had walked into the valley to face a giant with little more than a sling.

Before the meeting ended, David was once more enlisted in the service of his king. This time he was not being regarded as a minstrel. He had proven himself on the battlefield and in a single act had become something of a national hero. Even though he was young, he was the kind of man other men would follow into battle. His act of heroism would inspire bravery in the hearts of those who marched under his command. Recognizing the value of having someone like David in his army, Saul immediately commissioned him as an officer.

As he had suspected, the soldiers placed under David's command enthusiastically supported the king's action. Serving under David made them feel like soldiers again. It was a feeling they had forgotten during the weeks they had listened to Goliath rant and rage. They were reminded of the reasons they had chosen to fight for their king and nation in the first place.

Saul's decision was popular not only within the army itself, but also among his own staff. Some must have remembered his service in Gibeah and perhaps felt bad for the way he had been dismissed when the Philistines invaded. Those who had not known him previously soon found him to be the kind of person people like to be around. It must have been difficult at times to distinguish if it was really David they found attractive, or the prestige associated with being in the presence of a national hero. Fortunately, in this case the two were not mutually exclusive.

GREAT LEADERS EARN CREDIBILITY WITH THE PEOPLE THEY LEAD

THE BONDING OF A NEW FRIENDSHIP

Twice now, Israel had faced the Philistines and earned a victory in spite of overwhelming odds. In each battle, a hero in Israel had emerged. In the pass of Michmash, Saul's own son Jonathan emerged as a national hero (1 Samuel 14:1-45). In the Valley of Elah, David, son of Jesse, likewise was recognized. It was inevitable that someday the two heroes of Israel would meet.

Jonathan initiated his meeting with David. As he had watched the events unfold that day, something had stirred deep within. He remembered a day when he too was prepared to take bold action in the name of Israel's God against the Philistines. They were days when his passion for God had burned hot and he was convinced "nothing restrains the LORD from saving by many or by few" (1 Samuel 14:6). It seemed so long ago now since he too had been consumed by the passion for God that he saw in David that day.

As he had watched his father work through his own spiritual turmoil, Jonathan was also affected. Although the family had never been known for its spirituality, it was clear that the religion of Israel was quietly being replaced in the palace by a spirituality that had more in common with the Philistines than with Moses. No doubt part of that shift was Saul's response to a growing rift with the prophet Samuel, but it was more than that. This more recent approach to spiritual things seemed to fit their family better.

Jonathan was not one to object to the shift he witnessed. He too had begun to drift, naming his own son in honor of the widely worshipped storm god, Baal (1 Chronicles 8:34). In watching his father's degeneration, it was hard not to become a little angry with and bitter toward Israel's God. How could He do this to the king He had selected? It just didn't seem fair. And so the drift had continued.

Jonathan had likely not realized how much his family's spiritual drift had begun to erode the values he held dear until he saw David challenging Goliath. A few years earlier, he would have been in David's place. He had taken on a whole garrison of Philistines with only the aid of his armor-bearer, but over the past six weeks, he had been as terrified of Goliath as every other man in his father's army. Where was the courage and bravery that was so much a part of how he defined himself? He had not been able to find it again until he saw it in David that day.

In the aftermath of the battle, Jonathan realized he owed David a great debt. David's heroism in the Valley of Elah had sparked something deep within Jonathan that he had not felt in a long time. As he reflected on what happened during the march back to Israel's camp, he surely realized that David had done more than simply ignite the spark of bravery again. David had helped him believe in God again. He had seen in David what he had not seen in his father for a long time – a willingness to take God at his word and act accordingly. If David could trust God after all that had happened, then maybe Jonathan too could believe again.

No wonder "the soul of Jonathan was knit to the soul of David" (1 Samuel 18:1). They were indeed kindred spirits. Others might see them as two heroes in a common cause, but both David and Jonathan knew that the bond between them was deeper than a couple of victories over the Philistines. They shared a common love for God and a belief that He could and would act on Israel's behalf.

At the initial meeting of Israel's heroes, a covenant was forged between Jonathan and David. In this partnership, each recognized and honored the greatness they perceived in the other. A covenant of this nature showed each one's commitment to look out for the welfare of the other. It expressed a bond of friendship far deeper than that which might normally develop between men working together for a common cause.

Jonathan's commitment to David was not merely an idle expression of words. Immediately he saw a need of David's that he could meet. Saul had just transformed David from a shepherd to a soldier. The robe and equipment of a shepherd had served David well, but a transition had begun that would never be reversed. Jonathan took his own robe, the robe of a soldier, and gave it to David. Although David had acquired the armor of Goliath, it would be of little practical use to him in battle. Jonathan had no doubt also acquired weapons from fallen Philistines that day. He took his old armor and passed that on to the new soldier.

GREAT LEADERS RECOGNIZE AND HONOR THE GREATNESS OF OTHERS

THE FALLOUT OF SUCCESS

David accepted Jonathan's gift and wore his new robe and armor with great pride. There had been a time in Israel when there were few swords in Israel. As he drew the sword of Jonathan out of its sheath and gazed upon it, he realized he now possessed one of the oldest swords in the land. It was this sword Jonathan had used to gain Israel's first great victory over the Philistines. Now it belonged to him, the one to whom Israel's most recent victory over the Philistines was attributed. But David knew better.

He had stood in the Valley of Elah that day and challenged Goliath in the name of the LORD of hosts. He had claimed that his victory over the giant would enable the whole earth to recognize "that there is a God in Israel" (1 Samuel 17:46). Under the unwritten rules of war widely practiced throughout that era, the victor had the right to plunder the victim. No one in Israel would deny David the right to Goliath's sword, but David believed it belonged to another. He had announced that day, "the battle is the LORD's" (1 Samuel 17:47). If it had been the Lord's battle, then it had also been the Lord's victory. David would accept the gift of Jonathan's sword, but the sword of Goliath would be given to God, its rightful owner. At his earliest convenience, he would place Goliath's sword into the hands of the priest.

Though young and promoted in rank beyond most men of his age, David exercised wisdom in his new role as military leader. Those under his immediate command were the first to recognize David's wisdom in decision-making, which most often resulted in victory on the battlefield. A series of victories over the Philistines confirmed that David's success in the Valley of Elah had not been a fluke. Morale grew strong again as the whole company enjoyed the spoils of the victor.

Victories on the battlefield were generally followed by parades in the capitals. These too helped boost morale among the troops. As the army followed their king into the city carrying the trophies of war, their wives and families would line the streets as part of the celebration. Although winning battles was the work of men in Israel, since Miriam had led the women of Israel in a celebration over the drowning of the Egyptians (Exodus 15:20), it had become customary for Israel's women to sing and dance in the streets as part of the victory parade.

In such celebrations, hyperbole was the order of the day. A victory over ten men was often a victory over hundreds by the time the songs were sung. Two victories in a row demonstrated that the army was now invincible. While everyone knew these celebrations tended to be somewhat exaggerated, no one really cared. The soldiers who won the victory were certainly not going to stop the celebration to correct the exaggerated perceptions.

David's status as a national hero, together with the successive victories of his men, gave them an honored place in the victory parade. They led other companies, following only the royal family and Abner, Commander of Israel's Army. They could hear the crowds celebrating the greatness of their king before they began singing of their triumphs. During one particular parade, what they heard must have caused them to swell with pride. "Saul has slain his thousands, and David his ten thousands" (1 Samuel 18:7). The women's praise of David was praise for the whole company. It was doubtful that any other fighting unit in Saul's army would hear themselves celebrated in contrast with the king himself.

But David's men were not the only ones who heard the women sing that day. When Saul heard the singing, those who marched closest to him could tell he was angry even before he spoke. As an officer in Saul's army, both David and Saul would have perceived David's victories to be part of Saul's victories. But that was not what the women's song had declared. David's victories were being described as ten times greater than those of the king he served. The implications were not lost on the already insecure king.

"They have ascribed to David ten thousands," he snarled to his closest advisors. "And to me they have ascribed only thousands" (1 Samuel 18:7). Saul thought this was an injustice as he paced in anger. Maybe this is what Samuel had warned him about following the battle against the Amalekites. "The LORD has torn the kingdom of Israel from you today, and has given it to a neighbor of yours, who is better than you" (1 Samuel 15:28). Could it be that David was the one who would take the kingdom from his grasp? What other explanation could there be?

Saul had elevated David to his prominent office in the military. It seemed like the right thing to do in light of David's display of heroism on the battlefield. Maybe Saul had acted too rashly. He would have to be more careful with David in the future. He was sure David's professed loyalty was a front to catch him off guard when a coup was finally attempted. Surely that had to be his ambition. Samuel had practically said so. "So Saul eyed David from that day forward" (1 Samuel 18:9).

GREAT LEADERS ALWAYS RUN THE RISK OF BEING MISUNDERSTOOD

THE RETURN OF A DISTRESSING SPIRIT

"And it happened on the next day that the distressing spirit from God came upon Saul" (1 Samuel 18:10). Months earlier, the king's closest advisors had made a decision to send David back to Bethlehem hoping that battling the Philistines would distract the king from his fits of melancholy. A series of military victories had buoyed the king's spirit and seemed to confirm their speculations. But the king's anger and bitterness toward David had once again cracked open the doorway for the dark, distressing spirit from God to manifest itself.

Just when they thought they had resolved that problem, it reared its ugly head again in the palace. Everyone knew what would follow. The king's wide mood swings would once again make governing the nation impossible. Something had to be done quickly to deal with the problem before it became unmanageable. They had handled it once before, but their minstrel was now a national hero, suspected by the king of plotting treason.

Saul's suspicions of David were not widely accepted among the palace staff. They knew that David's could have used his knowledge of the king's former condition to provoke a successful coup, had that been his goal. The fact that he had maintained their confidence likely convinced them they were right about David in the first place; he could be trusted. But would a national hero be willing to play his harp for his broken king?

When approached about the urgent situation, David wasted no time in agreeing to help. As an officer in Saul's army, he had sworn loyalty to his king and agreed to serve him as best he could. He, like everyone else, had assumed that meant he would fight the king's battles. When Saul commissioned David, the king's greatest enemy was the Philistines. Now, that enemy was a distressing spirit. "So David played music with his hand, as at other times" (1 Samuel 18:10).

GREAT LEADERS ARE WILLING TO ADJUST TO SERVE WHERE THEY CAN BE MOST EFFECTIVE

The problem with Saul had become worse, and this situation was not "as at other times." The control this distressing spirit held over the king was more intense than it had been previously. He was consumed with anger and rage against David, yet at the same time he was also terrified of his young officer. Even in his unbalanced state, Saul could discern there was something different between him and David. "Saul was afraid of David because the LORD was with him, but had departed from Saul" (1 Samuel 18:12).

The Spirit of God had been responsible for Saul's initial success as king (1 Samuel 11:6). It was bad enough that Spirit was gone from him, but to see the same Spirit at work in the life of David was threatening.

Ironically, what Saul saw in David was consistent with his own blessing of David in the Valley of Elah. When he realized David could not be dissuaded from fighting Goliath, he had said, "Go, and the LORD be with you" (1 Samuel 17:37). What bothered Saul most about David now was that the Lord was indeed with David in everything he did.

> ### GOD'S ANSWER TO SAUL'S PRAYER
> "Go, and the LORD be with you" (17:37).
> The LORD was with him (18:12).
> The LORD was with him (18:14).
> The LORD was with David (18:28).

Afraid and intimidated by David, Saul felt he had to do something. He would not easily relinquish his grasp on the kingdom. As he stood listening to David play his harp, he realized he was holding a spear. Impulsively, he took aim and hurled the spear toward David. "I will pin David to the wall!" he thought as the weapon left his hand (1 Samuel 18:11). But as the spear made its way toward its intended target, David saw the danger and quickly moved out of the way. Realizing it was no longer safe to remain in the room, he quickly left the king alone.

David's escape from certain death caused Saul's fear of David to increase. What if David sought revenge for what Saul had attempted? The king would not let that happen. He issued orders to block David's access to the palace and promoted David to a higher rank within his army. With David's new responsibilities, he would be on the battlefield more often. While Saul's actions were designed to make him more secure, had he realized their effect he may have wondered about his decisions. David's new responsibilities resulted in increased exposure to the general population. As a result, "all Israel and Judah loved David, because he went out and came in before them" (1 Samuel 18:16).

Whether in the palace or among the public, in times of conflict or peace, David continued walking with God. Even though he found himself in the place where his boss liked him better dead, he realized he was safest in the presence of God. As a shepherd years earlier, he had learned how important it was that he always stay close to his Shepherd. Even when walking "through the valley of the shadow of death, I will fear no evil," he had concluded. "For You are with me; Your rod and Your staff, they comfort me" (Psalm 23:4). He would continue to depend upon that comfort in the days ahead as he walked with his God.

GREAT LEADERS WALK WITH GOD REGARDLESS OF WHERE HE TAKES THEM

A ROYAL WEDDING IN GIBEAH

Frustrated with his failure to eliminate David, Saul came up with another idea. It was time for him to find a husband for his oldest daughter, Merab. Believing that no man in Israel would turn down the opportunity to marry into the royal family, Saul told David, "here is my older daughter Merab; I will give her to you as wife. Only be valiant for me, and fight the LORD's battles" (1 Samuel 18:17). To those who witnessed that conversation, it would appear Saul was prepared to reconcile his differences with David. Saul, on the other hand, had an ulterior motive.

Despite the tendency of the times to glamorize war and celebrate great military victories, Saul had been king long enough to know there was a darker side to conflict. Great victories were often won at the cost of many fallen soldiers on the battlefield. There was no way to accurately predict who might fall in battle before the battle began, but it was reasonable to assume that the more time a soldier spent in the heat of the battle, the more likely that soldier would fall victim to the enemy. If Saul could not destroy David himself, he would entrust that task to his enemy, the Philistines. After all, Saul reasoned, David's good fortune would not last forever.

While David was honored by the king's offer, he expressed his own unworthiness to be part of the royal family. "Who am I, and what is my life or my father's family in Israel, that I should be son-in-law to the king?" (1 Samuel 18:18). This may have been David's polite way of accepting the king's offer and being able to continue fighting the Philistines. But when the time came for Merab to be married, "she was given to Adrielthe Meholathite as wife" (1 Samuel 18:19).

Although the Philistines had not yet killed David, Saul soon learned of a situation he was sure would accomplish his goal. He had been so focused on marrying his oldest daughter according to the custom of that time; he had not noticed that his younger daughter was definitely interested in David. Perhaps the feelings were mutual. But Saul's failure to follow through on his previous offer meant David was unlikely to take him seriously if he tried that approach again.

Saul gathered some of his closest advisors to enlist their help in his new plot. It was customary for a man to present a girl's father with a dowry (gifts) when he took her as his wife. Normally, the dowry required to marry a king's daughter would have been very large. But in David's case, Saul was prepared to make an exception. The servants were given a message to pass on to David. "The king does not desire any dowry but one hundred foreskins of the Philistines, to take vengeance on the king's enemies" (1 Samuel 18:25). Saul was certain that putting David against those odds would certainly result in his death at the hands of the Philistines.

When David learned the price for marrying Michal and

becoming the king's son-in-law, he was pleased. There was a time limit to the offer, but one he felt he could meet. The only thing he found disagreeable was the dowry price itself. David felt it was too little for such a woman as Michal. "Therefore David arose and went, he and his men, and killed two hundred men of the Philistines. And David brought their foreskins, and they gave them in full count to the king that he might become the king's son-in-law" (1 Samuel 18:27).

Once again, David had somehow escaped one of Saul's plots. In light of the situation, there was little else the king could do but give Michal to David as his wife. David's incredible victory over tremendous odds once again demonstrated that God was with David. As Saul saw how much his daughter loved her new husband, the inner unsettled feeling continued to grow stronger. "So Saul became David's enemy continually" (1 Samuel 18:29).

David continued serving in Saul's army as a respected commander in the ongoing war against the Philistines. He continued walking in wisdom in all of his dealings with others, friend or foe. It seemed that Saul's hostility had given him new insights into how to respond to life's situations. "And so it was, whenever they went out, that David behaved more wisely than all the servants of Saul; so that his name became highly esteemed" (1 Samuel 18:30).

THE GROWING WISDOM OF DAVID
David . . . behaved wisely (1 Samuel 18:5).
David behaved wisely in all his ways (18:14).
He behaved very wisely (18:15).
David behaved more wisely than all the servants of Saul (18:30).

GREAT LEADERS EXERCISE WISDOM IN THEIR ACTIONS

A TEMPORARY RECONCILIATION

Ever since the day he first heard the women of Israel singing David's victory song, Saul's fear of David had intensified. It had prompted him to action several times, but each attempt to end David's life failed to achieve the desired result. David's continual survival only confirmed his suspicions that he was the one who would seize Saul's throne from his grasp. His fear of David was quickly becoming irrational.

> ### THE GROWING FEAR OF SAUL
> Saul was afraid of David (1 Samuel 18:12).
> He was afraid of him (18:15).
> Saul was still more afraid of David (18:28).

Perhaps he had been too subtle. Saul reasoned that David survived because he had left too much to chance. With his new position as the king's son-in-law, David was more of a threat than he had even been before. The time had come for more direct action. Saul gathered his inner circle of advisors together and issued new orders. David must be killed. He was assigning this task to his most trusted servants.

At least one member of that group begged to differ with their king. The bond of friendship between Jonathan and David had grown deeper since their covenant established after their first meeting. When Jonathan left Saul's planning session, he quickly found

David and warned him. "My father Saul seeks to kill you. Therefore please be on your guard until morning, and stay in a secret place and hide. And I will go out and stand beside my father in the field where you are, and I will speak to my father about you. Then what I observe, I will tell you" (1 Samuel 19:2, 3).

David appreciated the warning and heeded it. He knew Jonathan was taking a significant chance on his behalf. This latest plot was only the most recent of a series of attempts on his life. He was not sure Jonathan would be successful in negotiating with Saul, but there really were no other options. He spent the night sleeping under the cover of the bushes growing at the edge of the selected field and arose with the sun the next morning, wondering what the day would bring.

Jonathan had carefully thought out his appeal to his father. As they walked through the field together, he began reciting David's virtues. He reminded his father that David had faithfully served him on every mission that had been assigned to him. Further, even before David was enlisted in Saul's army, he had risked his life against Goliath. In the process, he had gained the victory that had begun Israel's most recent succession of victories against Philistine forces.

Jonathan spoke passionately in defense of his friend. His argument was persuasive. As his son recounted the events of recent months, it became clear to Saul that David was a loyal subject. He was certainly not a threat to the throne. "So Saul heeded the voice of Jonathan, and Saul swore, 'As the LORD lives, he shall not be killed'" (1 Samuel 19:6).

This was exactly what Jonathan needed to hear. Looking across the field, he signaled for David to come out from his hiding place and his relationship with Saul was reconciled. Although he had been badly treated by his father-in-law the king, David understood that the real enemy was the Philistines to the west. If Saul would let him, he would continue serving in Israel's army. So it was that David "was in his presence as in times past" (1 Samuel 19:6).

GREAT LEADERS PURSUE PEACE OVER CONFLICT WHENEVER POSSIBLE

A NIGHT ON THE EDGE

Unfortunately the reconciliation between Saul and David was short lived. Before long, war with the Philistines erupted again. Once again, David led his men into battle and returned to the capital victorious. And once again, David's success marked a return of the distressing spirit. David's music was the only thing that seemed to ease these situations, so he was again asked to lay down his sword and pick up his harp.

The last time David had agreed to help in this way, Saul had attempted to kill him. When he was controlled by the distressing spirit, this danger always existed. But much had happened since that time. David was now part of the royal family by marriage and his previous problem with the king had been resolved through the intervention of Jonathan. But, as he sat playing his harp for his king, he quickly learned that Saul still harbored ill feelings toward him. Once again Saul hurled a spear at David, intending to pin him to the wall. Again David escaped successfully and slipped out of the palace into the night.

He had not been in his home long when he noticed soldiers gathering in the street. As he made out the features of those standing in the shadows, he realized these were not men in his regiment coming for his protection. There could only be one other explanation. These men had been sent by Saul to guard the house. David knew what would come next. In the morning, he would be arrested on made-up charges, publicly humiliated, and probably executed. He had escaped danger in the palace and had come to what he thought was a secure place, his home. Now his home was a holding cell, a place to remain until he was taken from there to the place of execution in the morning.

What David saw through his window terrified him. "At

evening they return, they growl like a dog, and go all about the city" (Psalm 59:6, 14). He had seen what a pack of wild dogs could do to a stray lamb that had wandered from the shepherd's protection. The very thought brought chills to his spine. But then he remembered those times when he had repelled dogs and other predators from his flock with a few rocks hurled by his sling. He too had a Shepherd, and to that Shepherd he called out.

"Deliver me from my enemies, O my God; defend me from those who rise up against me. Deliver me from the workers of iniquity, and save me from bloodthirsty men" (Psalm 59:1, 2). As he prayed intently, he remembered those nights in the pastures near Bethlehem. He could still hear the echo of the dogs he had driven from his flock. "They wander up and down for food, and howl if they were not satisfied" (Psalm 59:15). Even as he prayed, he trusted that somehow God would come to his aid in the midst of his desperate situation.

GREAT LEADERS TURN TO GOD FOR HELP IN THE MIDST OF DESPERATE CIRCUMSTANCES

Although David longed for relief from Saul's relentless attempts to destroy him, his prayer that night revealed a peaceable attitude toward the one who was the source of so much anxiety in his life. "Do not slay them, lest my people forget," he prayed (Psalm 59:11). While he must have realized that Saul must die before he could fulfill his destiny and become Israel's king, David had already decided that death would not come to Saul by his hand. This was a commitment that would be tested in the years to come, but a commitment he would keep.

Still, David called out to God to intervene in his situation that night. "Scatter them by Your power, and bring them down, O Lord our shield" (Psalm 59:11). He had no other defense but God and could rely only on God to defeat those ready to take him. Even if somehow he could have gotten a message to his loyal troops, their intervention that night could have sparked a civil war in the capital. Although he did not know how God intended for him to become king, he was not sure that war was the preferred means.

Even though he had not yet ascended to the throne, the people he would someday rule were foremost in David's thoughts. He pleaded with God to eliminate his enemy, but to do it in a way that all might "know that God rules in Jacob to the ends of the earth" (Psalm 59:13). However God chose to work this night, the story must be told to others so that God would be glorified in all He did on David's behalf. If his people could see the hand of God at work, he knew they would have greater confidence in God and attempt great things for His glory.

GREAT LEADERS CONSISTENTLY LOOK FOR WAYS TO INSPIRE THOSE WHO FOLLOW THEM

Even as he cried out to God, David realized that God would indeed keep him safe this night. "But You, O LORD, shall laugh at them; You shall have all the nations in derision" (Psalm 59:8). As a new calmness began to sweep over his spirit, he prayed, "I will wait for You, O You his Strength; for God is my defense. My God of mercy shall come to meet me; God shall let me see my desire on my enemies" (Psalm 59:9, 10). The anxiety now passed, he looked up to the heavens through his window.

Why hadn't he thought of this earlier? As he looked into the overcast sky, he noticed how dark the city had become. Even with men on the street, David realized he could escape under the cover of darkness. With the assistance of Michal, he tied several sheets together and quietly climbed out the window. Those guarding the house were so intent on watching the door they did not notice the man in the shadows making his way out of the city.

When David was gone, Michal pulled the sheets back into the house. She grabbed one of her idols and laid it in a bed that could be seen from their front door. She placed goatskin over the head of the idol that was close to the color of her husband's hair. She convinced herself that they could not tell the difference from a distance. Then she took the crumpled sheets David had used in his escape and piled them around and over the idol. As she gazed over her handiwork, she thought she might believe it was David herself had she not known better.

As David left the city, he breathed a deep sigh of relief. He did not anticipate the soldiers attempting to arrest him until morning. That gave him several hours to put as much distance between him and the city as possible. He picked up his pace, still not sure where he was going. As he thought over the events of the last hours, his heart began to fill with praise and thanksgiving to God for His answer to prayer.

"But I will sing of Your power; yes, I will sing aloud of Your mercy in the morning; for You have been my defense and refuge in the day of my trouble. To You, O my Strength, I will sing praises; for God is my defense, my God of mercy" (Psalm 59:16, 17).

GREAT LEADERS RECOGNIZE GOD CAN CHANGE THE INEVITABLE FOR HIS GLORY AND THEIR GOOD

THE INVASION OF RAMAH

When Saul's men finally entered the house to arrest David, Michal claimed he was sick in bed and could not go with them. Glancing over her shoulder, the commanding officer of the arrest party could see David sleeping under the blankets. Perhaps concerned for the health of their king, they returned to the palace without their prisoner and explained that he was sick.

Saul immediately recognized the opportunity that lay before him. If David was too sick to get out of bed, he would be too sick to defend himself or escape from Saul's attack. "Bring him to me in the bed," Saul commanded, "that I may kill him" (1 Samuel 19:15). It was only when the arrest party returned to David's home a second time that they discovered they had been deceived. By that time, David was far out of Saul's grasp.

David found himself in a new and difficult situation. He had faced dangers before, but even in dangerous situations there was always a place of refuge. As a shepherd watching sheep at night, he knew a large campfire would keep wild animals away. As a soldier on the battlefield, he knew he could find refuge in the security of his camp or a nearby fortress. But where could he be safe when the king himself wanted him dead? Surely Saul would think of looking for him in all the obvious places. As he considered the circumstances, there was one man David thought might be able to guide him through this difficult situation.

Samuel was the respected prophet of the age. He heard from God at a time when it seemed few were spiritually in touch with their Maker. It had been Samuel who had anointed him, claiming that God had set him apart to be Israel's king someday. In the aftermath of his victory over Goliath and his subsequent military victories against the Philistines, David had come to believe that the prophecy was beginning to be fulfilled. But what was he to think now? If he hadn't climbed out of the window, he probably would not be around to do anything by now. With nowhere else to turn, David made his way to Ramah, the home of Samuel.

When the two men met, David recounted all that had taken place. As he heard the story unfold, it became clear to Samuel that David needed a safe place to stay. He invited the future king to be his guest in the nearby village of Naioth. Living under the same roof as the prophet provided David a unique opportunity to glean wisdom from this older man of God. Samuel had learned much about life and Israel in his many years of ministry. He had also learned much about God and His ways. During their time together in Naioth, the prophet who had anointed David to office was able to equip him through daily instruction to better serve in that office.

GREAT LEADERS TURN TO OTHER GREAT LEADERS FOR GREAT COUNSEL

When Saul learned of David's hiding place, his suspicions were confirmed. David's presence in Samuel's home was all the evidence he needed to prove that the two men were conspiring together to overtake the kingdom. Samuel was an old man and well respected throughout Israel. To take action against the prophet would have been political suicide. But David was another matter. After all, if the two were conspiring together, David was the one being groomed to take the throne. If Saul could eliminate David, he could maintain his grasp on power.

Once again Saul sent out a group to arrest David. They made their way to the village determined not to be deceived again. As they approached the city, the troops saw Samuel in the midst of a group of prophets who were prophesying. Then quite unexpectedly, the troops felt a strange sensation pass over them. "The Spirit of God came upon the messengers of Saul, and they also prophesied" (1 Samuel 19:20). Unable to complete their mission, the men returned to Gibeah and attempted to explain why they had failed their king.

Still intent on eliminating his rival, Saul quickly organized another group to finish the mission the first group had failed to complete. But when they arrived at their destination, the same thing happened to them that had happened to the first group. A third arrest party was sent out to do the job, and once again history repeated itself. Frustrated with the failures of his staff, Saul decided to take matters once again into his own hands.

This time, Saul himself led the arrest party. When they arrived at Ramah, they made their way to the city well. In any city in Israel, the well was always the best place to gather information. As he asked about the whereabouts of Samuel and David, he soon learned they were in Naioth. After confirming the information, he and his men began the final leg of their destructive mission. Saul knew it was only a matter of hours before David would be his prisoner. By the time they returned to Gibeah, David would be eliminated and Saul could once again feel secure on his own throne.

Despite Saul's four attempts to kill David in Naioth, he remained there with Samuel, confident of God's protection over him. He was aware there was danger, but also sensed that God would ensure that his destiny would be realized. He recognized that the safest place he could ever be was in the midst of the will of God.

GREAT LEADERS EXPERIENCE GREAT SECURITY WHILE IN THE MIDST OF GOD'S WILL

Saul had not gotten far on the journey to Naioth when something began to happen. "Then the Spirit of God was upon him also, and he went on and prophesied until he came to Naioth in Ramah" (1 Samuel 19:23). When he finally came into the presence of Samuel, "he also stripped of his clothes and prophesied before Samuel in like manner, and lay down naked all that day and all that night" (1 Samuel 19:24). As much as he tried, neither the king nor those sent on behalf of the king could resist the working of the Spirit of God.

Those who witnessed this remarkable act could surely not help but notice the irony of the situation. Saul had come to Ramah intending to seize David from Samuel and destroy him. Now he lay naked before the prophet prophesying under the power of the Spirit of God. Once again, people in Israel asked, "Is Saul also among the prophets?" (1 Samuel 19:24).

CHAPTER FOUR

WHEN FRIENDS STEP IN TO HELP

1 Samuel 20:1-22:23; Psalms 56; 34; 142; 57; 52

The feeling of relief David felt leaving Gibeah and Saul's guards behind passed when he realized Saul had found him in Ramah. Despite the divine intervention that had prevented his arrest four times while in Samuel's care, the fear in his heart grew. As he became increasingly concerned for his own well being, his irrational fear motivated him to leave the security of Ramah and to take action that placed him and others in significant danger. Not until other people lost their lives due to his actions did David realize what he had done, and returned to the place of abiding trust in God. It all began with a trip back to Gibeah.

AN APPEAL TO A TRUSTED FRIEND

In his desperation, David appealed to Jonathan for help. He remembered Jonathan's intervention earlier and assumed that he, as Israel's crown prince, would be aware of the present danger to his life. "What have I done?" David asked him, wondering what had brought about this change in behavior by Saul. "What is my iniquity, and what is my sin before your father, that he seeks my life?" (1 Samuel 20:1). If he could identify the offense, then maybe he could once again reconcile with the king.

Following Jonathan's previous intervention, Saul realized a

strong bond of friendship had developed between his son and David. Knowing his son to be a man of character, one who would not betray a friend, Saul had chosen not to inform Jonathan of this plan to kill David. As far as Jonathan knew, the reconciliation he had effected between his father and friend was continuous. David's claims to the contrary were hard to believe. Jonathan had seen no evidence of hostility on the part of his father. At this point, David appeared to be a little paranoid. Jonathan's first impulse was to deny that any problem existed.

"You shall not die!" he responded emphatically. "Indeed, my father will do nothing either great or small without first telling me. And why should my father hide this thing from me? It is not so!" Jonathan concluded (1 Samuel 20:2). In preparing his son to some day rule over Israel, Saul had brought Jonathan into his inner circle, making him part of the decision-making process. Jonathan's involvement in the affairs of the kingdom fell just short of co-regency. In his mind, there was no way he would not be aware of the kind of situation David was describing.

David was not convinced. He suggested Saul was deliberately hiding his actions against David from Jonathan because he knew of their bond of friendship. He continued to insist that his life was in grave danger. "There is but a step between me and death," he claimed (1 Samuel 20:3).

The suggestion of a conspiracy of silence did little to convince Jonathan of David's claim. On the contrary, it only confirmed Jonathan's prior assessment of the situation. David was obviously scared, even panicked. Jonathan realized there would be no way to reason with him while he was consumed with an irrational fear. The best thing he could do for David as his friend would be to help calm him down by alleviating his fears. Jonathan was not certain what steps would best accomplish this goal; he offered to let David set the agenda. "Whatever you yourself desire, I will do it for you," he offered (1 Samuel 20:4).

Years later David's son, Solomon, would write about friendship, noting that, "Two are better than one, because they have a good reward for their labor. For if they fall, one will lift up his companion. But woe to him who is alone when he falls, for he has no one to help him up" (Ecclesiastes 4:9, 10). In many respects, Jonathan's friendship with David illustrates the essential character of a true friend.

GREAT LEADERS NEED GREAT FRIENDS WILLING TO STAND WITH THEM REGARDLESS OF THE CIRCUMSTANCES

DAVID'S PLAN

The feast of the New Moon would begin the next day. It was customary for families to celebrate that feast together. As the king's son-in-law, David would be expected to be part of the celebration in the palace. If David's seat were empty at the table, there would be no way Saul and others would not notice. David proposed that he hide in the fields for three days until the feast ended, and that Jonathan evaluate his father's response to David's absence to confirm or deny David's claim.

Jonathan would be in grave danger if Saul thought he was harboring a fugitive. The king would have taken his son's life on an earlier occasion had his army not objected over his planned actions. David had considered this and suggested a cover story he hoped would be credible. David was also the son of Jesse and it would be reasonable for him to return to Bethlehem occasionally to celebrate the feast with his father's family. If Saul were to ask Jonathan about David's absence, David urged him to lie and claim he was involved in an annual sacrifice and family feast in Bethlehem.

David had obviously given this plan some thought. Still convinced David's fears of Saul were unfounded, Jonathan saw this ploy as an opportunity to convince David of his error in judgment. For the sake of his friend's sanity, Jonathan would follow this plan. He agreed to participate and assured David of his continued loyalty. "If I knew certainly that evil was determined by my father to come upon you, then would I not tell you?" he asked (1 Samuel 20:9). This really was not a question, as the answer was obvious to both men.

David had forgotten to figure out how he would get a report from Jonathan, giving Jonathan the opportunity to further calm his friend's fear. He took David back to a familiar field to hide. It was here Jonathan had previously intervened with Saul on David's behalf and reconciled the two men. Jonathan apparently hoped the memories of that previous occasion would assure David of his security. Pointing to the place David had hidden previously, he urged him to hide there again. Jonathan agreed he would return within three days to confirm or deny David's version of events.

David's wild claims and Jonathan's reluctance to believe him had placed a strain on their relationship. David seemed calmer now than when they first met, but who knew what ideas might come into his head as he spent up to three days alone in the field thinking about what was happening in the palace? The last thing he wanted was for David to become so paranoid that he would run before Jonathan could return from his mission. Before he would leave David, he knew there was something he could do to assure his friend further.

The strategy agreed upon by David and Jonathan could only work in the context of the trusting relationship the two men shared. "So Jonathan made a covenant with the house of David, saying, 'Let the LORD require it at the hand of David's enemies'" (1 Samuel 20:16). By being proactive in reaffirming his loyalty to David, Jonathan could only hope David would continue trusting him to demonstrate that loyalty in the next few days.

Consumed with an irrational fear, David had run from the safety and security of Samuel and God's continued protective intervention in Ramah. He had run to, if David's claims were true, what may have been the most dangerous place for him to be in all Israel. If he ran again, there was no way of knowing where he might be found.

Jonathan could not risk his friend reacting that way while he hid and contemplated the situation. Therefore, "Jonathan caused David to vow, because he loved him; for he loved him as he loved his own soul" (1 Samuel 20:17). He knew David well enough to know that he would not break such a strong commitment.

GREAT LEADERS HAVE GREAT RELATIONSHIPS THAT SHAPE WHO THEY BECOME

THE FEAST OF THE NEW MOON

As Jonathan prepared to leave David, he once again reviewed the plan to assure David he understood what needed to be done and committed himself to their course of action. He would attend the Feast of the New Moon in the palace and watch Saul's response to David's absence. If David's absence became an issue, he would intervene on David's behalf and claim that he had been released from the palace feast to celebrate with his family in Bethlehem. When the feast ended on the third day, Jonathan would return to the field and reveal his findings through an agreed-upon signal. As the night of the new moon was the darkest night of the month, it would be easy for David to continue to hide.

Israel measured time using a lunar calendar, which measures months in terms of the cycle of the moon. The appearance of the new moon, on the evening when the moon is completely dark and not visible in the sky, marked the beginning of a new month. The twenty-eight days following this night marked the waxing and waning of the moon. In an agricultural society, this was the most practical way of measuring time. Moon cycles remain a key factor in forecasting weather patterns for preparing almanacs.

The Gentile nations surrounding Israel were driven by fear to offer sacrifices to their gods on the evening of the new moon. As they watched the moon decrease in size in the fortnight following the full moon, the shaman, or priest, claimed that the gods were angry and were bringing their world to an end. On the evening of the new moon, sacrifices would be offered to appease the angry gods. The appearance of a slender crescent in the sky the next night confirmed the shaman's power with the gods and increased their control over the people.

The Feast of the New Moon was also an integral part of Israel's worship calendar, but for a completely different reason. This feast was an expression of faith in God rather than fear of Him. Israel's worldview was based on an understanding that God created the moon and other celestial bodies "for signs and seasons, and for days and years" (Genesis 1:14). They viewed the presence of the moon as an expression of God's faithfulness to His covenant with them, His chosen people. Believing God would never break His covenant promises, expressions like "as long as the sun and moon endure" (Psalm 72:5) and "until the moon is no more" (Psalm 72:7) became ways of describing "forever." As a people in covenant relationship with God, the ongoing presence of the moon was a confirmation that God would continue honoring His covenant with them. "It shall be established forever like the moon, even like the faithful witness in the sky" (Psalm 89:37).

As expected, Saul celebrated the feast with the leaders of his army and David's absence was noted. "Nevertheless Saul did not say anything that day, for he thought, 'Something has happened to him; he is unclean, surely he is unclean'" (1 Samuel 20:26). There were many reasons why David might miss the feast, but as Saul thought about it, the most obvious was uncleanness. Many things could make a man unclean and therefore disqualify him from a religious celebration for a day, including having sexual relations with his wife (Leviticus 15:16-18) or touching a dead body in a recent battle (Numbers 6:9-12).

When David was also absent on the second day of the feast, Saul's curiosity got the better of him. As he looked around the table at those gathered for the feast, he realized that Jonathan would most likely know better than anyone else where David was. Turning to his son, Saul asked, "Why has the son of Jesse not come to eat, either yesterday or today?" (1 Samuel 20:27). Saul's question was reasonable, and Jonathan responded with what he thought was a reasonable answer, the one he and David had earlier agreed upon. However, from that point on, there was nothing reasonable about the night's feast.

Fathers have a way of seeing through their children's attempts to deceive them. There was something about Jonathan's response that alerted Saul and convinced him his son was not being completely honest with him. Maybe the answer sounded a little too practiced to be true. It may have been that in his pursuit of David, Saul had gathered intelligence from Bethlehem and already knew who was and was not attending the feast in that community. As he listened to his son's attempt to deceive him, the king was filled with rage and lashed out in a verbal attack.

"You son of a perverse, rebellious woman! Do I not know that you have chosen the son of Jesse to your own shame and to the shame of your mother's nakedness? For as long as the son of Jesse lives on the earth, you shall not be established, nor your kingdom. Now therefore, send and bring him to me, for he shall surely die" (1 Samuel 20:30, 31).

Saul's response must have taken Jonathan by surprise. He had been convinced David was wrong in his claims that Saul had a royal plot to take his life. Saul's decision not to raise the issue of David's absence the preceding night probably reassured Jonathan that his initial supposition had been right. Now his father's sudden outburst of anger showed him that he had been wrong all along. He had not counted on this response and struggled to find an appropriate answer.

This was not the first time Saul had determined to kill David. On a previous occasion Jonathan had been able to convince his father that David was no real threat. Maybe he could do it again. Appealing to his father, Jonathan asked, "Why should he be killed? What has he done?" (1 Samuel 20:32). Even as he spoke the words, he realized these were the questions David had asked him only days earlier. If he could find the cause of this recent break in the relationship, he felt he could once again mediate the dispute and reconcile his friend to his father.

While Jonathan's intent was good, trying to reason with individuals who are reacting at an emotional level does not usually produce the desired result. Saul was in no mood to be reconciled with. "Then Saul cast a spear at him to kill him" (1 Samuel 20:33). As Jonathan saw Saul hurl the spear at him, he realized he would not be able to change his father's mind. He managed to duck out of the line of fire, but not before he too began to burn with anger. His father was committed to killing his friend and had attacked his own son publicly among his peers. Jonathan stormed out of the room, too angry to even consider eating. As he lay in his bed that night, he knew what he must do next.

GREAT LEADERS SURROUND THEMSELVES WITH FRIENDS WILLING TO PUT THEMSELVES IN HARM'S WAY IN ORDER TO PROTECT THEM

The next morning, Jonathan took his bow and a young boy with him to practice his archery in the field where he had left David hiding. After releasing several arrows from his bow, he sent the boy to find them. As the boy looked for the arrows, Jonathan raised his bow once more and sent another arrow to a destination beyond the original target area. No one witnessing the action recognized it as a signal to David. Only two men understood the message that had just been communicated.

When the lad returned, Jonathan sent him back into the city with his weapons. It would not be long before he would also have to appear in the city, but he needed to take time to see his friend one more time. In light of what he had experienced at the feast the night before, Jonathan realized that apart from some kind of divine intervention, this could be the last time they would be together.

With heavy hearts the two men embraced and wept.

From the day they met, Jonathan and David had formed a deep bond that nothing and no one could break. The two men enjoyed being in the company of each other more than doing anything else. Now, that was no longer practical. As much as Jonathan wanted to continue having David close, he realized that would not be in David's best interest. At the same time, his father had made it clear that protecting David was not in Jonathan's best interest. But if he was going to be a true friend, he knew he had to release David into the care and keeping of God. (Psalm 46:1)

"Go in peace," he urged, "since we have both sworn in the name of the LORD, saying, 'May the LORD be between you and me, and between your descendants and my descendants, forever'" (1 Samuel 20:42). Knowing Jonathan was right, David left the field where he had been hiding in search for another safe refuge. Jonathan knew he had done the right thing, but his heart continued to ache as he made his way back into the city.

GREAT LEADERS HAVE FRIENDS WHO WILL MAKE HARD DECISIONS FOR THE BENEFIT OF THEIR FRIEND

A MEETING WITH THE PRIEST

His meeting with Jonathan had confirmed David's worst fears. Saul was intent on killing him and not even the intervention of the crown prince could sway him from that goal. Previously, Saul had enlisted the aid of his closest advisors in an attempt to destroy the son of Jesse. Because Jonathan had been excluded from the present attempt, David now had no idea who he could trust. Instinctively, he made his way to Nob, the home of the priests. Perhaps he could learn more by consulting the Urim and Thummim.

The Hebrew words "Urim" and "Thummim" literally mean "light" and "perfection," referring to one of several ways God communicated His will and revealed truth during Old Testament times. The priest's garment incorporated a breastplate that included twelve stones, one for each of the tribes of Israel. The name of a tribe was engraved on each stone. Together, the tribe names provided all but four letters in the Hebrew alphabet. Some Bible teachers believe the "perfection" referred to a thirteenth stone engraved with the remaining four letters. When the priest called upon God, a light was placed under the breastplate; it is believed that light would highlight various letters to spell out God's message to His people. (See Exodus 28:30; Leviticus 8:8; Deuteronomy 33:8; Ezra 2:63; Nehemiah 7:65.)

As David got closer to Nob, he began to have second thoughts. Jonathan's earlier insistence that Saul was not plotting to kill him meant the plot had not been widely publicized. Certain individuals of influence were no doubt involved, but Saul's current animosity toward David was not yet widely known. This created a new dilemma for the young warrior. Had the priest been enlisted in this plot? If so, he had to be careful what he said. If not, would he be any more likely to believe David's story than Jonathan had just days earlier? Uncertain of what he was going to face, he made his way to meet Ahimelech the priest with caution.

David's reputation was widely known throughout Israel. He had often been seen leading his troops into battle or returning with them to distribute the spoils of war. Military leaders always traveled with their troops, so David's appearance without his men was obviously outside the norm. Something was not right, and Ahimelech found it difficult to hide his alarm. He couldn't help but ask, "Why are you alone, and no one is with you?" (1 Samuel 21:1).

The question put David in an awkward position. He could see the fear in Ahimelech's eyes, but had no idea what that meant. Perhaps the priest knew of the plot against David and was surprised to see him alive. If so, David needed an explanation that would convince Ahimelech that Saul had everything under control. As he thought quickly, he remembered the king had tried to kill him previously by sending him on a covert mission against the Philistines.

"The king has ordered me on some business, and said to me, 'Do not let anyone know anything about the business on which I send you, or what I have commanded you'," he explained. This helped him past one hurdle, but he knew he still had to explain why his men were not with him. "I have directed my young men to such and such a place," he added (1 Samuel 21:2). If he convinced the high priest the mission was highly secretive, he could get away with being deliberately vague. As he watched Ahimelech's response, it was clear the priest believed his lie. It was also clear that David would not, under the circumstances, be asking the priest to consult the Urim and Thummim.

David asked for bread and was given some of the showbread baked daily for use in the tabernacle. As he accompanied the priest to get the flat bread commonly eaten throughout Israel, he noticed a familiar face. Doeg, an Edomite, was one of Saul's chief herdsmen. While he could not be certain what Ahimelech knew or did not know, it was highly unlikely that Doeg was unaware of Saul's plan. Suddenly he realized he had nothing with which to defend himself. He would not put it past Doeg to do Saul's work and take his body back to Gibeah for reward.

"Is there not here on hand a spear or a sword?" David asked the priest. No sooner had he asked the question than he realized his previous lie was beginning to unravel. What kind of soldier goes out on a covert mission without his weapons? Again, he had to think fast. "For I have brought neither my sword nor weapons with me, because the king's business required haste," he explained (1 Samuel 21:8). Even as he said the words, the excuse sounded weak. Fortunately, the priest was not a man of war and was not very likely to suspect the deception.

There was little need for weapons in the tabernacle. Even if they had been available, it was unlikely any of the priests would have known how to use them. Their unique role in Israel's worship meant they were exempt from military service. When they did accompany troops into battle, it was to pray, offer sacrifices and lead in the worship of God. Yet, ironically, there was one sword in the tabernacle that day; a sword David himself had presented as an offering to God following his victory over Goliath in the Valley of Elah.

"The sword of Goliath the Philistine, whom you killed in the Valley of Elah, there it is, wrapped in a cloth behind the ephod," Ahimelech noted (1 Samuel 21:9). He explained that was the only sword available, but David was welcome to take it if he wished. As he looked at the wrapped sword, he remembered how it felt in his hand that day so long ago. It was like no other sword he had seen before or since. Even the thought of holding it in his hand again encouraged his spirit. It did not take long for David to decide to accept this sword.

With the sword of Goliath in hand, David felt invincible for a moment. The iron weapon was probably the best in Israel, but in his hands it was more than just a great sword. He could not help but remember how God used him and a slingshot to destroy the mighty giant. As he carried the sword and bread away and continued his journey, his chances of surviving this present crisis were becoming more positive in his own mind. He was not yet sure how, but just as God had delivered him from Goliath, he was certain that Saul would not be successful in his plan.

GREAT LEADERS RELY ON PAST VICTORIES FOR ENCOURAGEMENT THROUGH A PRESENT CRISIS

RUNNING INTO THE ARMS OF THE ENEMY

Armed with the sword of Goliath, David must have begun feeling a little invincible. Doeg the Edomite was no longer the threat he had been earlier. He managed to leave the city without incident and tried to convince himself everything would be all right. Still, he had a nagging feeling that something was wrong, but just wasn't sure what it meant. One thing he was sure of was the need to get far from Saul's reach. Looking at the sword once again in his possession, he came up with an idea.

Saul might comb all Israel looking for him, but there was one place David knew he would not find him. If David lived among the Philistines, he would be far from the reach of Saul. Without thinking through the idea thoroughly, he made his way to Gath, Goliath's hometown. Some Bible teachers believe he intended to live among the Philistines incognito; however, he was discovered, captured and taken to the Achish, the king of Gath (Psalm 56). Others believe David originally intended to appeal to Achish for protection from Saul (1 Samuel 21:10). David may not have completely thought out his plan any farther than getting out of Israel. Regardless of his intention, soon it became apparent this had not been a good idea.

David was not in the city long before he began hearing Philistine soldiers talking among themselves. "Is this not David the king of the land? Did they not sing of him to one another in dances, saying: 'Saul has slain his thousands, and David his ten thousands?'" (1 Samuel 21:11). David remembered the song well. It was the same song that had awakened Saul's jealous streak, the song that marked the beginning of his troubles with Saul. Until he heard the soldiers talking, he had not been aware how well known he was among the Philistines.

Holding the sword of Goliath, he realized he should have anticipated problems in entering this city. Goliath, the Philistine champion, was no doubt a hometown hero in Gath. His father and brothers still lived in the city. Just as his defeat of Goliath had been widely celebrated in Israel, the residents of this city would no doubt remember the name of the young shepherd who had caused their shame. Once again terror gripped his heart. As he prepared to meet Achish, he knew he had to act quickly.

Although life had been difficult in Israel with raiding Philistine parties constantly attacking, David's long experience in dealing with this nation was about to become an advantage. Most Israelites understood the Philistine culture as much as they did their own. And one thing David knew was that Philistines lived in constant fear of evil spirits. It was widely believed among the Philistines that when an evil spirit possessed a man, he would go mad. They also thought that if someone got too close to such a mad man, the spirit might leap from his body to their own.

As David waited for the king, he began an act he hoped would save his life. He began scratching himself and drooling. Then he began scratching other things as he contorted his face. His actions were designed to communicate what he could not say. He wanted the Philistines to believe he was possessed and had been driven mad. It was the only way he could think of to guarantee that they would keep their distance so he could escape. He was not sure he could convince everyone with this act, but that was not necessary. David knew there was only one person he really needed to convince.

When Achish arrived and saw David's actions, he reached the desired conclusion. He had not expected to see David in such a state. Why hadn't someone warned him of the danger before he had agreed to come? Enraged, he turned to his men and shouted, "Look, you see the man is insane. Why have you brought him to me? Have I need of madmen, that you have brought this fellow to play the madman in my presence? Shall this fellow come into my house?" (1 Samuel 21:14, 15).

Once Achish had declared David mad, no Philistine soldier would consider any other explanation. As concerned for their own state of mind as they were for that of their king, they quickly opened the gates in hopes that David would wander away from the city. David continued the act long enough to leave Gath and travel far enough from the city to guarantee his safety. Only then did his act of madness turn into an expression of worship and thanksgiving to God for His miraculous deliverance.

GREAT LEADERS FIND CREATIVE WAYS TO RESOLVE PROBLEMS, EVEN IF THE PROBLEM IS OF THEIR OWN MAKING

David wrote two psalms in the context of his experience in Gath. The first begins with a description of the conditions that drove him to make the unwise decision to go to Gath in the first place. "Be merciful to me, O God, for man would swallow me up; fighting all day he oppresses me. My enemies would hound me all day. For there are many who fight against me, O Most High" (Psalm 56:1, 2). As Saul plotted to destroy David, he had come to feel there was no one left he could trust. In this circumstance, he came to the realization that there was always One in whom he could trust. "Whenever I am afraid, I will trust in You" (Psalm 56:3).

The second psalm linked to this experience in Gath celebrates the deliverance he experienced. Although David had come up with the idea of feigning madness, it is clear he viewed his deliverance as an act of God. "I sought the LORD, and He heard me, and delivered me from all my fears," he confessed (Psalm 34:4). "This poor man cried out and the LORD heard him, and saved him out of all his troubles" (Psalm 34:6). In light of that deliverance, David declared, "I will bless the LORD at all times; His praise shall continually be in my mouth. My soul shall make its boast in the LORD; the humble shall hear of it and be glad. Oh, magnify the LORD with me, and let us exalt His name together" (Psalm 34:1-3).

THE CAVE OF ADULLAM

David left Gath grateful for the intervention of God, realizing that living among the Philistines was not an option at this point. Although he knew Saul was determined to destroy him, others did not. If he stayed in Philistia, he would be viewed as one of Saul's spies and treated accordingly. He returned to Judah, but was not certain it was wise to be seen by many people. He needed time alone to work through the situation he was facing. He made his way to the Cave of Adullam, a reasonably secure hiding place in the forest. It was a place he could live in obscurity and provide for his necessities by hunting in the wilderness. This might not be a permanent solution, but it would do for now.

One advantage of living alone in a cave was having time to seriously think things through. David had not had such a luxury since the day he conquered Goliath in the Valley of Elah. There were times when he longed for the lengthy hours he had enjoyed when he watched his father's sheep. He missed meditating on the things of God around him; the life of the rising leader had been busy! Now, alone in the cave, he had time to more carefully consider what was happening.

"I cried out to the LORD with my voice; with my voice to the LORD I make my supplication," he wrote during those days. "I pour out my complaint before Him; I declare before Him my troubles." Life looked very dark and difficult as he considered his situation. But then he began to realize something. "When my spirit was overwhelmed within me, then You knew my path" (Psalm 142:1-3). Although David did not understand why things had happened as they had, he knew the One who did understand.

His prayers in those early days in the cave were prayers of desperation. He felt lonely and abandoned. "In the way in which I walk they have secretly set a snare for me. Look on my right hand and see, for there is no one who acknowledges me; refuge has failed me; no one cares for my soul" (Psalm 142:3, 4). He cried out to God from the deep sorrow of his heart, not knowing what was going to happen. Still, during that time he was reminded of a truth he had known for years. God knew his path. Just has he had led his father's flocks through the wilderness of Judea years earlier; it was now time for him to let God lead him. He remembered the day Samuel poured the anointing oil over his head. A promise had been made then that would not be broken. He was not sure how God would resolve this one, but he knew He would. "Bring my soul out of prison," he prayed, "that I may praise your name; the righteous shall surround me, for You shall deal bountifully with me" (Psalm 142:7).

The Scriptures are not clear how long David stayed alone at the Cave of Adullum, but he stayed long enough. He was alone at the cave long enough to turn to God for help rather than continuing to depend upon the efforts of friends, religious leaders and foes. He was alone long enough to realize God was still in control and knew the path that would be taken. He was alone in the cave long enough to begin trusting again that God could turn even this experience into one that would ultimately glorify Him.

GREAT LEADERS UNDERSTAND THE VALUE OF SOLITUDE

NEW RULES FOR THE NEW REGIMENT

God soon answered David's prayers from the cave in a most unusual way. Saul's plot against David could not remain hidden for long. Nor could David live within Judah long without someone recognizing him. The first to respond to the news that David had returned was his own family. "When his brothers and all his father's house heard it, they went down there to him" (1 Samuel 22:1). The petty differences that had seemed to divide the family for years were now set aside. Those who knew David best were the first to declare their allegiance to him. In doing so, they must have realized they were risking not only their lives but also the wealth and influence that had taken them years to accumulate.

Others began taking sides in the growing conflict between David and Saul. "And everyone who was in distress, everyone who was in debt, and everyone who was discontented gathered to him. So he became captain over them. And there were about four hundred men with him" (1 Samuel 22:22). While this new following may have encouraged David, it also made hiding from Saul harder. Concerned that his aging parents may not be able to travel as fast as younger members of the new community, David made arrangements for them to live in Moab, the ancestral homeland of his great-grandmother, Ruth.

David's experience at the cave had brought him back to the place of dependence upon God. His appeal for God's mercy in his life and the lives of those for whom he was now responsible was a request from a heart of faith rather than a cry of desperation. "For my soul trusts in You; and in the shadow of Your wings I will take my refuge until these calamities have passed by" (Psalm 57:1). His commitment to trust God alone was soon put to the test.

With a small army now loyal to him, David considered the option of establishing his own stronghold, a city with walls that would provide him and his people security and could be defended against any attack launched by Saul. Initially he established a stronghold in the territory of Moab. From that location, he could see any invasion force coming long before it reached the city. After all he had done recently to escape Saul's plot, it felt good to be able to rest soundly at night. But before long, the prophet Gad came to David with a message from the Lord. God wanted David to leave the stronghold and return to Judea. From a security perspective, the idea did not seem to make sense.

However, by now, David had another perspective. He understood God was the Most High, Possessor of heaven and earth. He had come to recognize that God "performs all things for me" (Psalm 57:2). While there were risks associated with this plan, he was prepared to trust God in this situation and stretch the faith of his people to do the same. He no longer had to worry about exalting himself to become king of Israel. God would take care of that. For now, he had a new theme. "Be exalted, O God, above the heavens; let Your glory be above all the earth" (Psalm 57:5, 11). This new regiment he was leading would learn the discipline of faith from his example.

GREAT LEADERS PUSH THEMSELVES AND THEIR FOLLOWERS TO ABANDON THE STATUS QUO FOR A HIGHER STANDARD

THE SLAUGHTER OF THE PRIESTS

It is easier to hide one man than to hide an army. David had not been back in Judah long before the news reached Saul. When the message arrived, Saul was shocked to hear that David was not only alive but had managed to raise an army of four hundred men. Enraged, he accused his servants of conspiring with David in exchange for a promised reward. He was still bitter that his own son had chosen to make a covenant with David. Now he was convinced that his closest advisors had become part of a conspiracy against his throne.

Saul's advisors knew just how unpredictable the king could be when he was filled with rage. The sight of him ranting about an alleged conspiracy as he stood in the shade of a tamarisk tree holding his spear must have brought a sense of terror to each one. They could only wonder which of them would be the target of the king's wrath. It was then that Doeg the Edomite spoke, recalling something he hoped would save him from harm.

"I saw the son of Jesse going to Nob, to Ahimelech the son of Ahitub," he reported. "And he inquired of the LORD for him, gave him provisions, and gave him the sword of Goliath the Philistine" (1 Samuel 22:9, 10). His slightly embellished story achieved its desired result. The angry king turned his paranoid attention from his circle of advisors to the priests of Israel.

When Ahimelech appeared before Saul, he was immediately accused of being part of a conspiracy against the throne of Israel. Samuel had earlier told Saul that he would be replaced, so it only made sense to the king that the priests would participate in this plot. Ahimelech denied any knowledge of or involvement in a plot, but

Saul had already made up his mind. He turned to his men and ordered them to kill the priests. But the soldiers of Israel "would not lift their hands to strike the priests of the LORD" (1 Samuel 22:17).

There was one man present who did not share the faith of the others, who also had good reason for silencing Ahimelech. In Doeg's effort to distract Saul's angry accusations from his advisors to the priests, he had claimed that Ahimelech had consulted the Lord on David's behalf (1 Samuel 22:10). Ahimelech had already denied doing that (1 Samuel 22:15). As long as the priest remained alive to tell the truth, there was a chance he might be believed and Doeg would be exposed as a liar. When given the opportunity to do so, Doeg killed not only Ahimelech, but eighty-five priests living in Nob. Only one priest, Abiathar, escaped with his life.

David's instinctive response when he learned of Doeg's action was outrage. "I knew that day, when Doeg the Edomite was there, that he would surely tell Saul," he claimed (1 Samuel 22:22). In a psalm he wrote in response to the news, he described Doeg as evil. "Your tongue devises destruction, like a sharp razor, working deceitfully. You love evil more than good, lying rather than speaking righteousness. You love all devouring words, you deceitful tongue" (Psalm 52:2-4). David remained confident that God would certainly judge Doeg for his actions.

But David also knew Doeg alone was not responsible for the death of the priests. His own actions had contributed to the situation. Looking back, he realized it had been unwise for him to go to Nob. To the only surviving son of Ahimelech, he confessed, "I have caused the death of all the persons of your father's house. Stay with me; do not fear. For he who seeks my life seeks your life, but with me you shall be safe" (1 Samuel 22:22, 23).

GREAT LEADERS
ACCEPT RESPONSIBILITY
FOR THE MISTAKES THEY MAKE
AND PROBLEMS THEY CAUSE

CHAPTER FIVE

WHEN THE DAYS ARE DARK AND THE YEARS GROW LONG

1 Samuel 23:1-28:2; 29:1-30:31; Psalms 11; 64; 7; 10; 13; 17; 22

Having broken free of the paralyzing fear that had clouded his judgment earlier, David began assuming increased responsibility for the welfare of others. Even though Saul was still pursuing him, he knew God had a greater plan for his life. The prophet Samuel had anointed him as Israel's next king. David had a deep and abiding conviction that the plan of God would not be hindered in his life.

In some respects, David was already acting like a king. Several hundred people, who were among those discontented with the status quo in Israel, had begun following David. Included in this group were prophets, priests and a small but efficient army. David's status had grown sufficiently enough for him to be able to make alliances with neighboring nations, as he had with Moab to ensure the care and protection of his parents. Even beyond his immediate following, others in Israel were beginning to look to him as their leader.

Not long after the lone surviving priest, Abiathar, joined David, news arrived that the people of Keilah were in danger. The initial report informed David that a Philistine group had invaded Keilah during the harvest and were robbing the people of their recently thrashed grain. This behavior was as typical of their Philistine neighbors as it had been of previous enemies of Israel throughout the rule of the judges. The conquering army was not so much interested in occupying new lands as they were in looting the land of anything they found valuable. Most often, this involved taking the new harvest along with the women and children, who became their slaves.

As the leader of the armed militia that was closest to Keilah, David was inclined to assume responsibility for the city's protection. But this time he would take nothing for granted. Before taking action on his own, he sought to determine God's will in this situation. When he asked, probably through the mediation of Abiathar, the answer of God was clear. "Go and attack the Philistines, and save Keilah" (1 Samuel 23:2).

Although David had broken free of his fear, his men were still afraid. When they learned of his intentions, they immediately objected. "Look, we are afraid here in Judah. How much more then if we go to Keilah against the armies of the Philistines?" (1 Samuel 23:3). It was bad enough having one enemy, King Saul. If they attacked the Philistines, they ran the risk of gaining another major enemy.

Knowing his men needed their confidence strengthened before going into battle, David once again took the matter to the Lord. While he may have consulted God privately when seeking His direction, he may have done it more publicly on this occasion. He already knew what God wanted him to do, but he also likely felt that his men needed to hear it for themselves. God's answer to David's question was clear and unmistakable. "Arise, go down to Keilah. For I will deliver the Philistines into your hand" (1 Samuel 23:4).

Assured of victory, "David and his men went to Keilah and fought with the Philistines" (1 Samuel 23:5). The raiding enemy party, which had probably invaded to loot the city, was defeated and lost many of the possessions that they had begun to steal. David and his men took away the Philistines' livestock, the symbol of their wealth and strength. Though raised by the Philistines, these animals would be used to strengthen the small growing army of David as they continued protecting Israel from her enemies, even as Saul still pursued them.

GREAT LEADERS DO NOT LET PERSONAL PROBLEMS DISTRACT THEM FROM THE TASK AT HAND

PURSUED IN THE WILDERNESS

It was not long before Saul learned that David had intervened to protect Keilah. Rather than acknowledge this victory as an act of loyalty, fighting the king's battle for him, Saul saw it as an opportunity to capture and destroy his rival. While living in the wilderness, David and his army had always had the advantage of mobility and were hard to track down. Now that they had attached themselves to a city, they would be easier to attack.

"God has delivered him into my hand, for he has shut himself in by entering a town that has gates and bars," Saul explained to his advisors (1 Samuel 23:7). Cities built walls as a defense against invaders, but the walls that kept the enemy out could also be used to keep the city people in. When fighting against a walled city, armies often laid siege and cut off supply lines going into the city. This took time, but as the city's reserves were exhausted, they often surrendered without a fight. Even when the end came in the form of a battle, the residents of the city were often demoralized and physically weaker when the fighting would begin.

Although Keilah was an Israelite city, Saul's hatred for David spilled over to the city. He assumed the people of the city would be loyal to David because of his intervention. Because he viewed David as his enemy, Keilah was now also an enemy of the state. Messengers were sent out with a call to arms and Saul's standing army was expanded to include soldiers from across the nation. Saul would take no chances this time. He wanted an army big enough to ensure that David would not escape.

GREAT LEADERS ARE OFTEN THE TARGET OF LESSER MEN

As the tension between Saul and David became more public, the people of Israel were becoming more aware that all was not well in Gibeah. David was widely popular in Israel as a military hero and some found it hard to believe that this loyal soldier had become a threat to national security. It is likely that news of David's intervention on behalf of Keilah had also been widely reported. As a result, when Saul issued his call to arms and announced his intention to lay siege of Keilah and capture David, some Israelis chose not to join Saul's army. Instead, they sent warnings to David to inform him of Saul's plan.

Despite all that had taken place, David remained loyal to Israel and her king. Saul's plans to attack an Israeli city in order to capture him created a situation David found difficult to understand. He knew he would have to respond, but he was unsure what that response ought to be. Desiring direction from God, he called on his new priest, Abiathar, and asked him to bring the ephod, the Urim and Thummin, that he had rescued during Doeg's attack on the priests.

As he considered the situation, David had several questions. Although there was no reason to doubt the sincerity of the messenger who had brought the warning of Saul's planned attack, the idea of a king attacking his own city was so strange he found it hard to believe. As he sought God, David prayed, "O LORD God of Israel, Your servant has certainly heard that Saul seeks to come to Keilah to destroy the city for my sake. Will the men of Keilah deliver me into his hand? Will Saul come down, as Your servant has heard? O LORD God of Israel, I pray tell Your servant" (1 Samuel 23:10, 11).

David did not have to wait long for his answer. "He will come down" (1 Samuel 23:11). When he asked again how the men of Keilah would react, God answered, "They will deliver you" into the hand of Saul (1 Samuel 23:12).

As difficult as it was to believe that Saul would attack, it must have been even more difficult to believe that the leaders in Keilah would betray David. It had not been that long since he had rescued the city from certain doom. But it was now apparent the city was unsafe for David and his men. He gathered his men and went to the Wilderness of Ziph. When Saul learned David had left Keilah, he aborted his planned attack. David's actions had, for the second time, saved the city that valued him so little.

GREAT LEADERS ARE SOMETIMES UNDERVALUED BY THOSE WHO OWE THEM MOST

THE ANGUISH OF ABANDONMENT

Any sense of relief David may have felt in leaving Keilah soon vanished when Saul learned of his new location. David and his men traveled from stronghold to stronghold in the forested region but they knew Saul was continually pursuing them. "Saul sought him every day, but God did not deliver him into his hand" (1 Samuel 23:15). There was little question now that Saul would not be satisfied until he stood over David's dead body.

Even though God was faithful in protecting David from Saul, the constant pressure of being pursued began to wear on David emotionally. The language of various psalms David wrote during this time reveals some of the struggles he faced under the circumstances. He wanted to trust God, but struggled with a real sense that his life was in constant danger. He cried out, "O LORD my God, in You I put my trust; save me from all those who persecute me and deliver me, lest they tear me like a lion, rendering me in pieces while there is none to deliver" (Psalm 7:1, 2).

When David did not experience the immediate relief he hoped for, he began wondering if he was responsible for the misfortune he was facing. Perhaps this was a judgment from God for something he had done. He continued praying, "O LORD my God, if I have done this: if there is iniquity in my hands, if I have repaid evil to him who was at peace with me, or have plundered my enemy without cause, let the enemy pursue me and overtake me; yes, let him trample my life to the earth, and lay my honor in the dust" (Psalm 7:3-5). If David was being judged, he wanted God to act quickly and take his life rather than allow his daily agony to continue. Christians must learn to be still and let God use situations to teach faith and obedience. (See Psalm 46:10; Hebrews11:6.)

As the days wore on, David began wondering if he was so distant from God that God was no longer even listening to his prayer. "Why do You stand afar off, O LORD? Why do You hide in times of trouble?" (Psalm 10:1) "How long, O LORD? Will You forget me forever? How long will You hide Your face from me? How long shall I take counsel in my soul, having sorrow in my heart daily? How long will my enemy be exalted over me?" (Psalm 13:1, 2) "My God, my God, why have you forsaken Me? Why are You so far from helping Me, and from the words of My groaning? O my God, I cry in the daytime, but You do not hear; and in the night season, and am not silent" (Psalm 22:1, 2).

Even though he was not sure God was even listening, David continued to cry out to God to intervene in his situation. "But You, O LORD, do not be far from Me; O my Strength, hasten to help me! Deliver me from the sword, my precious life from the power of the dog. Save me from the lion's mouth and from the horns of the wild oxen!" (Psalm 22:19-21). "Consider and hear me, O LORD my god; enlighten my eyes, lest I sleep the sleep of death; lest my enemy say, 'I have prevailed against him'; lest those who trouble me rejoice when I am moved" (Psalm 13:3, 4).

GREATLEADERS STRUGGLE WITH EMOTIONS COMMON TO ALL PEOPLE

Despite all the apparent evidence to the contrary, God had not abandoned David nor was He deaf to the repeated prayers that had been uttered. He responded to David in his darkest hour by sending his dearest friend to minister in David's life. "Then Jonathan, Saul's son, arose and went to David in the woods and strengthened his hand in God" (1 Samuel 23:16). It was the last time the two men would meet and there are no detailed records of what transpired that evening, but David understood the visit was a direct answer to prayer. "You have answered me," he cried out to God (Psalm 22:21).

Jonathan's encouragement enabled David to adjust his focus and begin completely trusting God again. He understood "The LORD is in His holy temple, the LORD's throne is in heaven; his eyes behold, his eyelids test the sons of men" (Psalm 11:4). With renewed faith he could pray, "Show Your marvelous lovingkindness by Your right hand, O You who save those who trust in You from those who rise up against them. Keep me as the apple of Your eye; hide me under the shadow of Your wings, from the wicked who oppress me, from my deadly enemies who surround me" (Psalm 17:6-9). Although the enemy still seemed to be closing in, David knew they would not achieve their goal. "But God shall shoot at them with an arrow; suddenly they shall be wounded. So He will make them stumble over their own tongue; all who see them shall flee away. All men shall fear, and shall declare the work of God; for they shall wisely consider His doing" (Psalm 64:7-9).

GREAT LEADERS HAVE GREAT FRIENDS WHO ENCOURAGE THEM IN THEIR FAITH IN GOD

A NARROW ESCAPE

David's renewed faith in God was not based on the circumstances he faced. Saul continued to pursue David with help from others who lived in the area. At some point following Jonathan and David's final meeting, the Ziphites sent a delegation to betray

David. "Is David not hiding with us in the strongholds in the woods, in the hill of Hachilah, which is on the south of Jeshimon?" they reported. "Now therefore, O king, come down according to all the desire of your soul to come down; and our part shall be to deliver him into the king's hand" (1 Samuel 23:19, 20).

Saul was understandably pleased with the offer but by now realized David and his men were extremely mobile. Before committing troops to pursue David in the Wilderness of Ziph, he asked the Ziphites to confirm David was still there. When they sought to confirm David's presence, they learned he was then in the Wilderness of Maon. Based on this more recent intelligence, Saul sent his troops in pursuit of David.

Before long, Saul's men found evidence of a recent camp and began pursuing the trail that would take them around the mountain to David. "Then Saul went on one side of the mountain, and David and his men on the other side of the mountain. So David made haste to get away from Saul, for Saul and his men were encircling David and his men to take them" (1 Samuel 23:26). With Saul's men so close, it seemed to be only a matter of time before David would be captured.

Ironically, it was the Philistines who indirectly rescued David. As Saul and his men were in close pursuit of David, a messenger arrived with news of a Philistine invasion. As much as Saul wanted to destroy David, he had no way of knowing just how close he was to achieving that goal. As king, he knew the threat to national security by the Philistines was a higher priority and must be dealt with. The Philistine invasion forced Saul to temporarily abandon his pursuit of David. David took this opportunity to relocate to an oasis called En Gedi.

WALKING AWAY FROM OPPORTUNITY

With six hundred men, plus their wives and children, now following David, it was becoming increasingly more difficult to keep hidden from Saul. Shortly after the battle with the Philistines ended, Saul received another report informing him "David is in the

Wilderness of En Gedi" (1 Samuel 24:1). Saul gathered three thousand of his best men and led them on a search and destroy mission to deal with David and his men once for all.

While traveling in the region, Saul halted his men near the mouth of a cave. As his men waited outside, Saul entered the cave alone to relieve himself. What he did not realize was that this was the very cave where David and his men had chosen to hide. Saul could not see David and his men hiding in the shadows, but they could see him and recognized him immediately.

David's men could not believe their eyes. There was no question that God had arranged this opportunity to end Saul's life so they could live in peace. They reminded David of God's promise to deliver his enemy into his hands and urged David to attack. Quietly, David crept toward the place where Saul had hung his robe and cut a piece of cloth from its edge. But when he did this, his conscience began to bother him. Turning to those closest too him, he said, "The LORD forbid that I should do this thing to my master, the LORD's anointed, to stretch out my hand against him, seeing that he is the anointed of the LORD" (1 Samuel 24:6).

David's reminder of Saul's unique office in Israel restrained his men from taking any further action. Silently they waited as Saul finished, put his robe back on and left the cave to resume his mission. Soon after, they watched and followed David as he too left the cave. From a safe distance, David called out to attract Saul's attention.

Once he was certain that Saul knew who he was, David relayed what had just happened. He once again declared that he had no malice toward the king and certainly did not want to do him any harm. He confessed to having cut Saul's robe and used that to demonstrate how he had not killed Saul when he had an opportunity to do so. He urged his king not to believe those who suggested otherwise and appealed for an end to their hostilities.

When Saul realized what had happened, he wept with remorse. Calling back to David he acknowledged, "You are more righteous than I; for you have rewarded me with good, whereas I have rewarded you with evil. And you have shown this day how you have dealt well with me; for when the LORD delivered me into your hand, you did not kill me" (1 Samuel 24:17, 18). Saul understood that this was not the way a man would treat someone he considered his enemy. He was convinced David meant him no harm.

Saul was also convinced that David was the one Samuel had spoken of as the next king of Israel. Now assured that David had no intent to take the kingdom by force, he asked him not to destroy his family or erase his name from Israel's memory. When David agreed, Saul called off the mission and the two went their separate ways.

GREAT LEADERS KNOW WHEN TO REFUSE TO TAKE MATTERS INTO THEIR OWN HANDS

THE END OF AN AGE

Saul had apparently been appeased, but David knew this change of heart might not last long. This was only the most recent of a long series of reconciliations between the two men. On each previous occasion, Saul had turned on David without warning. In light of this, it seemed unwise for David to return to Gibeah with his men – Saul's next unprovoked attack on David could likely spark a civil war within the capital itself. That was the last thing the nation needed. So, David and his men returned to their wilderness stronghold. There was still an enemy to fight, one that could best be fought from their position on the frontier.

Philistine raiding parties often invaded the border area to take what they wanted from defenseless farmers. This danger led to an emerging security industry involving various militia groups protecting farmers from raiding parties. In appreciation for the protection, the farmers responded by giving the militia men a portion of their harvest or the increase of their flocks. This arrangement provided David with an opportunity to both protect Israel from the enemy and provide for the physical needs of his men and their families.

The truce with Saul removed significant pressure from David and his men. No longer were they concerned about betrayal nor did they have to watch over their shoulders to ensure their own people were not pursuing them. The new situation enabled them to focus more clearly on the enemy. Regular patrols were dispatched throughout the region in search of Philistine raiding parties. The few battles fought by David's men served as a deterrent to other groups who may have wanted to plunder the region. As a result, farmers throughout that region prospered by cutting their losses. It seemed everything was working out well for everyone.

But a shadow on the horizon was brought to David's attention when a message arrived from Ramah. Samuel the prophet had died. He had emerged as God's spokesman during one of Israel's darkest hours and had, more than any other person, been responsible for the restoration of Israel as a nation. News of his death drew large crowds to Ramah to mourn his passing and remember his contributions to the nation.

While others mourned, the pain David felt was more personal. He remembered the day he had been called in from the fields; the day Samuel had poured oil over his head; the day the Spirit of God came upon him and he learned he would be Israel's next king. So much had taken place since that day that David still struggled to understand. On several occasions, he had consulted with Samuel who had helped him make sense of these things. Now Samuel was gone, and David was alone.

The passing of Samuel marked a significant transition in the history of Israel. The nation had been born under the strong leadership of Moses and possessed the land under Joshua's capable leadership. Since that time, judges had ruled the nation. Samuel was the last of the judges. He had anointed Israel's first king, but had remained as an unsolicited advisor, hoping to ease Israel's transition into the monarchy. That king had neither always responded well nor valued the assistance that was offered. Samuel had also anointed Israel's second king. Israel was now entering into a new age of being governed by a monarchy.

GREAT LEADERS ARISE IN THE MIDST OF TRANSITIONAL TIMES

ABIGAIL

One of the businessmen whose flocks were protected by David and his men was a man named Nabal. His extreme wealth was reflected in the three thousand sheep and one thousand goats he owned. Like others in the region, he prospered as a result of David's protection, having had no losses throughout the season. He was married to a wise and beautiful woman named Abigail, but Nabal himself had earned a reputation as a harsh and evil man. His dealings with David and his men illustrated just how foolish Nabal could be.

As Nabal and his shepherds gathered to shear the sheep, David sent ten men to meet with Nabal and accept whatever gift he wished to offer. The shearing of sheep was a festive time of year, as owners celebrated their profits and gave gifts to those who had helped make that profit possible. But when David's men arrived at this festival, Nabal refused to acknowledge David or give him any part of the profits being shared with others. His attitude toward David's men was so severe that he intimidated his own shepherds, who were grateful for David's protection.

When his men reported back to David, he was incensed at the insult. He knew if a rich man like Nabal challenged him, it might not be long before others also refused to acknowledge David's efforts on their behalf. "Every man gird on his sword," David called out in anger (1 Samuel 25:13). He was about to do something he might have thought unwise if he were not so enraged. His men armed themselves and four hundred followed David into battle against Nabal. David was leading his men into a battle against his own people. He left two hundred men behind to guard their supplies in the event the conflict spread and others attacked David.

But Nabal was not the only one in the family with the authority to express thanksgiving for services offered. When one of the shepherds reported what had taken place to Abigail, she realized there was no time to waste. She had seen her husband deal with others and knew he had a way of antagonizing those who support- ed him. Therefore, without consulting him, she quickly gathered bread, fruit and meat from her own supplies and had her servants load them on donkeys. Perhaps in order to avoid any further mis- understanding, she decided to travel with her servants to present this gift to David and his men.

Abigail intercepted David and his men as he was making his way to attack Nabal. Despite her family's wealth, she humbled her- self before David and asked his forgiveness for the previous insult. She offered the gift of supplies she had brought as an expression of appreciation for David's protection of their flocks. Further, she expressed her conviction that God would establish David's rule even though he was then living in exile and being pursued by Saul. She pointed out that, in light of his future reign, attacking Nabal might be a source of grief as he assumed the throne.

Few leaders of that era considered women wise enough to be consulted in making decisions, but David set aside a cultural value of the day and recognized the good judgment Abigail expressed. Further, he publicly acknowledged her wisdom when he said, "Blessed is the LORD God of Israel, who sent you this day to meet me! And blessed is your advice and blessed are you, because you have kept me this day from coming to bloodshed and from aveng- ing myself with my own hand" (1 Samuel 25:32, 33). David acknowledged that he would have destroyed Nabal and his family had Abigail not wisely intervened.

GREAT LEADERS NEED WISE COUNSEL FROM MANY SOURCES TO AVOID MAKING UNWISE DECISIONS

Abigail returned to her husband to find him drunk from

overindulging during the celebrations. She waited until morning when he was sober to discuss what she had done to protect the family. When he learned of the situation, he was shocked and it appears that he went into cardiac arrest. He hung on the edge of life for ten days before dying.

News spread fast in the region and it was not long before David learned of the circumstances of Nabal's death. Once again he realized how much he owed Abigail, whose intervention had prevented him from angrily taking revenge. It was now clear that God had taken vengeance on Nabal and there had never been any need for David to act. Knowing that widows often struggled, and recognizing the value of having a wise and beautiful woman like Abigail as a wife, he sent a messenger with a proposal of marriage. Abigail accepted and became one of David's wives.

REFUSING TO HARM THE LORD'S ANOINTED

Although Saul had not recently been actively pursuing David, relations remained cool between the two men. As he had reluctantly welcomed David into his family by marriage, Saul annulled David's marriage to Michal and married her to another man. To challenge this decision would have only further angered Saul. When David married Ahinoam of Jezreel and Abigail, his actions may have been perceived as an insult to the royal family.

Once again the Ziphites approached Saul with intelligence concerning David's location. David had been spotted in their territory, in the same area he had been previously. Remembering how close he had been to capturing David with the Ziphite's help previously, Saul once again gathered three thousand of his best troops for another search and destroy mission led by Abner, Commander of Saul's army. They made their way to the hill of Hachilah opposite Jeshimon and set up their base camp.

But Saul was not the only one with a well-established intelligence network. David was informed of Saul's approach and was able to view Saul's camp from his vantage point in the wilderness. As he looked over the situation, it appeared the army had no organized defense. Abner had failed to assign sentries and post watches, confident there was no danger nearby. At sunset, the men bedded down for the night and the camp was left completely unprotected.

David knew that six hundred men advancing on the camp would run the risk of waking some of Saul's men, but he thought a couple men might be able to enter and exit the sleeping camp unnoticed. Together with Abishai, David went into Saul's camp, "and there Saul lay sleeping within the camp, with his spear stuck in the ground by his head. And Abner and the people lay all around him" (1 Samuel 26:7).

This was the second time Saul was helpless and within David's reach. As on the previous occasion, Abishai's first thought was that this was God's way of letting David end the hostility between the two men. Further, Abishai was willing to act on David's behalf and guaranteed success if allowed to do so. "God has delivered your enemy into your hand this day. Now therefore, please, let me strike him at once with the spear, right to the earth; and I will not have to strike him a second time!" (1 Samuel 26:8).

Once more, David refused to let one of his men harm Saul. "Do not destroy him; for who can stretch out his hand against the LORD's anointed, and be guiltless? As the LORD lives, the LORD shall strike him, or his day shall come to die, or he shall go out to battle and perish. The LORD forbid that I should stretch out my hand against the LORD's anointed" (1 Samuel 26:9-11).

GREAT LEADERS REMAIN TRUE TO THEIR PERSONAL VALUES AND ACT ACCORDINGLY

Remembering how his first refusal to kill Saul had resulted in a temporary truce, David knew it would be valuable to have some proof he had been present in the camp. He ordered Abishai to take Saul's spear and water jug and the two quickly made their way out of the camp. They traveled to the top of a distant hill where they could be seen and heard, but not pursued, by Saul and his army.

From their secure vantage point, David called out to Abner so the whole camp could hear. He accused Abner of dereliction of duty, a crime worthy of death, for failing to adequately defend his king. Saul recognized the voice soon after David began speaking. David held up Saul's spear and water jug, both of which had been near his head the night before. He did not need to explain how they were now in his possession – all who were present knew that it meant he could have killed Saul if he had wanted to do so.

Once again, Saul recognized he had misjudged David's motives and confessed the error of his ways. David agreed to return the water jug and spear to a young soldier if he came alone to David's camp. The exchange was made, and Saul returned to the palace. Once again the two men had been reconciled, but in light of their history, no one was certain how long this truce would last.

THE PHILISTINE ALLIANCE

The long struggle in the wilderness was beginning to wear on David. Even though he had some degree of liberty at the moment, he knew that would not last long. There had been many close calls and narrow escapes in the past and he wondered if he could count on many more in the future. He was getting tired of being pursued and wondered how much longer he could endure. As he considered his options, he knew as long as he remained in Israel, the risk remained.

The one place Saul was not likely to look for him was in the Philistine territory. He had run to Achish in fear and despair years earlier to no avail, but much had changed since then. Previously, David was alone, recognized as the champion of Israel and the son-in-law of Saul. The rift between the two men was now widely known and, even though he led a small army, he was no longer viewed as a threat to the Philistines. Achish now assumed David viewed Saul as an enemy in light of the events of recent years, and he welcomed him to his city. Eventually, David and his men were given the city of Ziklag for their home.

As David suspected, when Saul learned that David had relocated into Philistine territory, he abandoned his pursuit. The last thing he wanted to do was to create a misunderstanding and start another war by moving his army into Philistine territory. Even if the Philistines realized the attack was against David and not them, Saul had no way of confirming whether a formal alliance had been made between David and any of the Philistine lords. If he had, an attack on David could plunge Israel into a war against the Philistines.

For David, living among the Philistines had its own challenges. Saul was getting old and David likely assumed it may not be much longer before his time would come to rule Israel. When that happened, many who served in his army would be elevated to prominent ranks within Israel's army. It was important that they continue fighting, but to attack a Philistine city would invoke the wrath of that nation upon him. Attacking cities in his homeland was not an option. While it might win him favor with the Philistines, it would undermine his authority when it came time to assume Israel's throne.

David came up with another plan. He would use Ziklag as his base of operations against Israel's enemies to the south. He would have specific targets in mind, but if questioned by the Philistines, he and his men would be deliberately vague and speak of the general direction of their raids. According to their preconceived perception that David was hostile toward Saul, they would likely assume he was attacking Judah.

There was one potential drawback in this plan. If they were not exhaustive in their attack, it was possible that an enemy who escaped could report David's activities to the Philistine authorities. Therefore, when David and his men attacked Israel's enemies, they were thorough. There would be no survivors to inform the Philistine leadership what he was doing. The only evidence a battle was even fought was the wealth that was accumulated. Those who saw this new wealth had no way of determining its source. Also, by sharing part of his wealth with the cities of Judah, the Philistines never realized just how extensive his campaigns were.

David's stay at Ziklag helped him prepare in two ways to rule Israel. First, he led a successful army into battle and gained the experience he would need to lead Israel's army as her king. Second, because the Philistines did not recognize David as a threat, he was able to learn much about that nation that would aid him in future battles with Israel's traditional enemy.

GREAT LEADERS USE PRESENT OPPORTUNITIES TO PREPARE FOR FUTURE ENDEAVORS

THE BURNING OF ZIKLAG

David's ruse at Ziklag worked so well that Achish believed David was among his most loyal warriors. Achish concluded David "has made his people Israel utterly abhor him; therefore he will be my servant forever" (1 Samuel 27:12). When the Philistines gathered in battle against Israel, Achish assumed David would serve on the battlefield along side him. It was the kind of invitation David could not decline. Not certain how he would resolve this obvious conflict of interest when the time came, David agreed to gather with the Philistines as they prepared for battle with Israel. If nothing else, he would gain valuable insight into the Philistines' preparations for conflict.

While Achish was convinced of David's loyalty, other leaders of Philistine cities were not. When they saw David and his men armed and in the midst of their battle camp, they objected to their presence. They expressed their anger toward Achish and ordered, "Make this fellow return, that he may go back to the place which you have appointed for him, and do not let him go down with us to battle, lest in the battle he become our adversary" (1 Samuel 29:4). They feared that David might reconcile with Saul at the expense of many Philistine lives.

Reluctantly, Achish met with David, explained the situation and asked him to return to Ziklag. As it was already late in the day, David agreed to leave the camp at dawn. As the sun rose over the horizon the next morning, he and his men began the journey back to Ziklag. They had extended their alliance with Achish without having to attack their own people. But when they returned to Ziklag, they discovered they would not be completely exempt from battle.

As David and his men journeyed to Shunem, the site of the Philistine camp, a raiding party of Amalekites had invaded the south and attacked Ziklag. Though no lives had been lost, they had taken all the women and children captive and burned the city to the ground. The anguish felt by the men was so intense upon their return, some even talked of stoning David for leading them to the Philistine camp and leaving the city defenseless. Even though David himself was also grieving the loss of his wives and people, he managed to encourage himself and look to God for guidance. Convinced he would recover everything they had lost if he pursued the Amalekites, he immediately led his men into battle.

By the time they came to the Brook Besor, about a third of his army was so exhausted they could travel no longer. They had marched from Shunem to Ziklag, experienced an intense emotional trauma, and headed off in pursuit of the Amalekites without taking time to get the rest they needed. Eager to quickly recover his losses, David left two hundred of his men at the brook and led the rest along what appeared to be the trail of the Amalekites.

Along the way, the men discovered the almost lifeless body of an Egyptian in a field. When they gave him food and water, something he had not had in three days, he revived and became a valuable source of intelligence. The Egyptian explained how his master had abandoned him to die three days earlier because he was sick. He confirmed that the group they were pursuing was the same party that had raided and destroyed Ziklag. The Egyptian slave also led David and his men to an open plain where the Amalekites had set up camp to celebrate their recent victories.

David and his men rested until twilight before launching their attack on the Amalekite camp. They fought through the night and into the next day. By the time the sun set again, everything that had been taken from Ziklag had been recovered unharmed. They also recovered much that had been taken from Judah, which had also been raided by these Amalekites. Only the four hundred Amalekites mounted on camels managed to escape David's attack.

As the group made their way back to Ziklag, some of David's men felt that the two hundred who remained at the brook should not be allowed to share in the spoils of war because they had not been on the battlefield. When David heard this idea being discussed, he objected immediately and insisted the spoils of war would be shared equally among all the men. "My brethren, you shall not do so with what the LORD has given us, who has preserved us and delivered into our hand the troop that came against us. For who will heed you in this matter? But as his part is who goes down to the battle, so shall his part be who stays by the supplies; they shall share alike" (1 Samuel 30:23, 24). As far as David was concerned, the spoils of war were a gift from God, not the achievement of soldiers. Therefore, all would share in God's bountiful goodness.

GREAT LEADERS RECOGNIZE THE CONTRIBUTIONS OF EVERYONE INVOLVED, EVEN THOSE BEHIND THE FRONTLINES

CHAPTER SIX

WHEN THE LIGHT AT THE END OF THE TUNNEL FINALLY BEGINS TO GLOW

1 Samuel 31:1-2 Samuel 2:32; Psalms 25; 35; 69; 109

Although based in Philistine territory, David and his men often journeyed home into Judea. Some trips into the territory may have been personal, to visit friends and family who remained in the traditional homeland. On other occasions, the trips may have served as regular patrols as part of Judah's defense. Regardless of the reason, these frequent journeys to Judea resulted in the strengthening of relationships of the people and elders of Judah with David and his men. When David's men traveled in Judea, they did so with great liberty and without fear of betrayal to Saul.

Even though circumstances made it impossible to live at home, David's love for his people never diminished. When he raided his enemies, it had been his custom to share the spoils of war with friends and family back home. He understood that some of his men had aging parents and other family members, who they would have helped provide for if they were free to work their farms in Judea. By sending part of the spoils of war home, his men were sharing their wealth with others in need.

When David returned to Ziklag, he sent some of the spoils to the elders of Judah. In each city, elders gathered at the city gate to make decisions concerning the welfare of their city. These men were chosen not only because of their age, but also because of the wisdom and character they possessed. By sending the spoils of war to these men, David recognized the social infrastructure of the community and could be certain the resources would be distributed where needed most. This was his primary concern in sharing the spoils of war.

This action did not go unnoticed in Judea. Each time a gift arrived, the elders and people knew David had won another of the Lord's battles against the enemies of Israel. In a nation surrounded by aggressive enemies with strong armies, being successful on the battlefield raised one's credibility as a leader. Also, the people knew that David had no obligation to share his spoils with them. They had seen Saul go to battle and increase his personal wealth. In their actions, the character of the each man was revealed. David's generous spirit further served to make him a more appealing leader in Judea.

GREAT LEADERS EXHIBIT GREAT GENEROSITY TOWARD OTHERS

THE FALL OF SAUL

While David fought the Amalekites to rescue those taken from Ziklag, Saul fought the Philistines. It was the last battle he would fight, ending with his death and the death of his sons. The final hours of Saul's tragic life reveal just how far he had wandered in his relationship with the God who had made him Israel's first king.

As the Philistine army gathered at Shunem in preparation for war, Saul responded by gathering Israel's army at Gilboa. With the two armed camps in close proximity to each other, it was easier for each side to gage how strong the enemy was. The intelligence gathered by Israel was not good news. The Philistine army was much larger than anticipated and better equipped for battle. "When Saul saw the army of the Philistines, he was afraid, and his heart trembled greatly" (1 Samuel 28:5).

Saul realized he was in deep trouble and needed divine intervention, but his actions in recent years had distanced himself from God. "And when Saul inquired of the LORD, the LORD did not answer him, either by dreams or by Urim or by the prophets" (1 Samuel 28:6). Just as Saul had ignored God's warnings repeatedly, so now God chose to ignore Saul's pleading.

In the past, when all else failed, Saul knew he could count on Samuel. Even when he did not like what Samuel said, he knew the prophet spoke the truth as God revealed it to him. However, the prophet was now dead and buried, no longer available to the king. But Saul thought he had a way to overcome this problem. He would speak to Samuel beyond the grave through the aid of a medium.

Occult activities were widely practiced in Canaan when Israel came into the land. God had repeatedly banned these practices from Israel in His law. "You shall not permit a sorceress to live" (Exodus 22:18). "Give no regard to mediums and familiar spirits; do not seek after them, to be defiled by them: I am the LORD your God" (Leviticus 19:31). "And the person who turns to mediums and familiar spirits, to prostitute himself with them, I will set My face against that person and cut him off from his people" (Leviticus 20:6). "A man or a woman who is a medium, or who has familiar spirits, shall surely be put to death; they shall stone them with stones. Their blood shall be upon them" (Leviticus 20:31). "There shall not be found among you anyone who makes his son or his daughter pass through the fire, or one who practices witchcraft, or a soothsayer, or one who interprets omens, or a sorcerer, or one who conjures spells, or a medium, or a spiritist, or one who calls up the dead" (Deuteronomy 18:10, 11).

Saul understood clearly what the law taught about consulting mediums. One of his early actions as king had been to apply this principle in Israel. "Saul had put the mediums and the spiritists out of the land" (1 Samuel 28:3). But over time, Saul's character had changed. He began with little compromises concerning the things he once believed and had come to the point that he was now prepared to engage in actions he once condemned.

As Saul changed his values, he also gathered around him those who shared his new views. Had he indicated a desire to consult a medium in his early reign as king, there would have been advisors who would have warned him of the danger and suggested a different course of action. Those men of courage and conviction were no longer part of Saul's inner circle. When he asked his servants, "Find me a woman who is a medium, that I may go to her and inquire of her," his servants responded, "In fact, there is a woman who is a medium at En Dor" (1 Samuel 28:7).

When Saul arrived at the medium's home, he made his request. "Please conduct a séance for me, and bring up for me the one I shall name to you" (1 Samuel 28:8). Even though Saul had disguised himself well, the medium was hesitant to comply fearing this might be a trap. "Look, you know what Saul has done, how he has cut off the mediums and the spiritists from the land. Why do you lay a snare for my life, to cause me to die?" (1 Samuel 29:9). Only when Saul assured her she would not be in danger did she agree to help.

While the occult practices involve demonic spirits to some degree, many occult practitioners are fraudulent and use various tricks to convince their gullible clients they have made contact with the dead. They would use vague statements to draw information out of their clients and then report that information back under the guise of being a message from beyond, thus earning an unwarranted reputation of being able to consult with the dead. The medium Saul consulted may have been such a con artist. Yet when she began this time, something happened that terrified her. Samuel actually appeared.

Saul calmed the panicking medium and urged her to continue. When she reported seeing an old man coming up out of the earth wearing a mantle, "Saul perceived that it was Samuel, and he stooped with his face to the ground and bowed down" (1 Samuel 28:14). When Samuel asked why he had been consulted, Saul cried out, "I am deeply distressed; for the Philistines make war against me, and God has departed from me and does not answer me anymore, neither by prophets nor by dreams. Therefore I have called you, that you may reveal to me what I should do" (1 Samuel 18:15).

Samuel was Saul's last hope, but the deceased prophet offered no hope at all. "So why do you ask me, seeing the LORD has departed from you and has become your enemy? And the LORD has done for Himself as He spoke by me. For the LORD has torn the kingdom out of your hand and given it to your neighbor, David. Because you did not obey the voice of the LORD nor execute His fierce wrath upon Amalek, therefore the LORD has done this thing to you this day. Moreover the LORD will also deliver Israel with you into the hand of the Philistines. And tomorrow you and your sons will be with me. The LORD will also deliver the army of Israel into the hand of the Philistines" (1 Samuel 28:16-19).

When Saul heard Samuel's message from God, he remained prostrate on the ground, possibly under intense conviction for his sin. He had no appetite for food and seemed to ignore everything else that was around him, laying terrified and shaking on the ground. Some Bible teachers believe this moment was Saul's final opportunity to repent and return to God, thus avoiding the inevitable judgment of God. The medium realized that if Saul repented, one of the first evidences of that repentance would involve her stoning. Scared, she pleaded for her life. "Look, your maidservant has obeyed your voice, and I have put my life in my hands and heeded the words which you spoke to me" (1 Samuel 28:21).

The medium knew she had to break this conviction from Saul before he repented, so she suggested he get up and eat. When he refused, his servants realized they too would be victims for their involvement with the medium if Saul repented. They urged Saul to rise and enjoy a meal before they left. Eventually, they convinced their king to get up. Together, Saul and his servants ate a meal of bread and beef before returning to the camp.

The next day, the battle proceeded just as Samuel had predicted. The Philistines gained the upper hand quickly and many in

Israel's army deserted under fire. When the enemy identified the royal family, they became the primary target of the fighting force. Saul's sons were among the first casualties of war. The king himself was wounded by an archer and began to bleed. When Saul realized his wound was fatal, he looked for a quick death. When his armor bearer refused to assist him, he took matters into his own hands and fell on his sword. When the Philistines discovered the bodies of the Royal Family the next day, they had them decapitated and hung them naked from the wall of Beth Shan as a final act of humiliation.

The Philistines boasted of their victory over Saul, sending the news throughout the whole land. It was not long before the news also became known in Israel. "Now when the inhabitants of Jabesh Gilead heard what the Philistines had done to Saul, all the valiant men arose and traveled all night, and took the body of Saul and the bodies of his sons from the wall of Beth Shan; and they came to Jabesh and burned them there. Then they took their bones and buried them under the tamarisk tree at Jabesh, and fasted seven days" (1 Samuel 31:11-13).

Three days passed before David learned of the outcome of the battle. A man arrived from Saul's camp with his clothes torn and covered in dust. This was a common expression of grief and mourning in Israel, so his very appearance indicated that he was bearing bad news. When David learned this man had escaped from the battle, he immediately asked him, "How did the matter go? Please tell me" (2 Samuel 1:4).

GREAT LEADERS ARE CONSISTENTLY CONCERNED FOR THE WELFARE OF THOSE THEY ARE CALLED TO SERVE

THE REPORT OF AN AMALEKITE

The man reported, "The people have fled from the battle, many of the people are fallen and dead, and Saul and Jonathan his son are dead also" (2 Samuel 1:4). The news was not what David had hoped to hear. Even though he was disturbed at the news that Israel had lost the battle with the Philistines, he was especially concerned about the report that Saul and Jonathan had been killed. He would not believe the report until he saw proof. When he asked the man for proof, he heard a slightly different account of the battle.

The man, who identified himself as an Amalekite, claimed to have been on Mount Gilboa by chance when he met Saul trying to escape from Philistine chariots and horsemen pursuing him. According to the Amalekite, Saul asked him, "Please stand over me and kill me, for anguish has come upon me, but my life still remains in me" (2 Samuel 1:9). The Amalekite then claimed he killed Saul, an act of mercy to end the life of a dying man.

By this time, the tension between Saul and David was common knowledge. With both Saul and Jonathan dead, the most likely choice for king in Israel was David. Knowing this, the Amalekite reported, "I took the crown that was on his head and the bracelet that was on his arm and have brought them here to my lord" (2 Samuel 1:10). He knew that having these symbols of power in his possession would make it easier for David to return to Israel and claim the throne.

As David looked at Saul's crown and bracelet, he knew these articles would not have been given up easily. They lent credibility to the Amalekite's claim that Saul and Jonathan were both dead. "Therefore David took hold of his own clothes and tore them, and so did all the men who were with him. And they mourned and wept and fasted until evening for Saul and for Jonathan his son, for the people of the LORD and the house of Israel, because they had fallen by the sword" (2 Samuel 1:11, 12).

While still grieving over Israel's loss, David met again with the Amalekite. It was ironic that the actions of Amalekites, a people Saul had been commanded to destroy, should result in both Saul's death and keeping David away from the battlefield. Still, David had one more question for which there could be no answer. "How was it you were not afraid to put forth your hand to destroy the

LORD's anointed" (2 Samuel 1:14)? Even though Saul's actions against David may have been motive enough to kill the king at the first opportunity, David repeatedly had refused to kill Saul or allow his men to do so on his behalf, because he respected him as the one God had called to be king.

No doubt, the Amalekite had not expected this kind of response from David. He thought he would be glad for the news and reward him as the bearer of glad tidings. But he would not be rewarded this day. Turning to one of his men, David ordered, "Go near, and execute him!" (2 Samuel 1:15). The order was quickly obeyed and moments later the Amalekite lay dead in a pool of his own blood.

GREAT LEADERS EXERCISE GREAT JUSTICE, FOLLOWING PRINCIPLES ABOVE EXPEDIENCE

WHAT REALLY HAPPENED TO SAUL?

Some people claim that having two biblical accounts of the death of Saul is an example of the Bible being inaccurate in recording history. However, there is overwhelming evidence to the contrary. The discoveries of archaeologists working in the Middle East over the past century have repeatedly confirmed the historicity of both the Old and New Testaments, even in cases where the biblical record was different from other histories of that time. Still, having two significantly different accounts of one event makes the Scripture's report worthy of a second look.

Some Bible teachers believe the key to harmonizing these apparently contradictory accounts is to view the second as an expansion of the first. In this approach, Saul would have been unsuccessful in taking his own life when he fell on his sword. His armor-bearer may have assumed the suicide attempt had been successful, thus he took his own life, but the Amalekite may have passed shortly after and found Saul wounded both by the archer and his own failed suicide attempt. Assuming the Amalekite's report was accurate, he would have realized there was no way Saul could survive much longer and so agreed to finish the task upon Saul's request. This explanation fits well with all the facts recorded in both accounts.

There is a second view held by some Bible teachers that also explains the differences in the two accounts. The Amalekite was simply a liar hoping to impress David by taking credit for something he had not done. Those who hold this view believe Saul was successful in taking his own life and that the Amalekite passed by later that day and found the king already dead. Perceiving an opportunity to impress David, he took Saul's crown and bracelet and made his way to Ziklag. He created the story on the way to further convince David of his loyalty.

In the event the second explanation is accurate, it might be argued that the Amalekite was executed for a crime he did not commit. David may have had his own doubts about the accuracy of some details in the Amalekite's account of the death of Saul. In his final words to the condemned man, David said, "Your blood is on your own head, for your own mouth has testified against you, saying, 'I have killed the LORD's anointed'" (2 Samuel 1:16). If the Amalekite's story was fabricated, David so valued truth and integrity that he held the Amalekite guilty of simply having professed to killing Saul.

GREAT LEADERS VALUE TRUTH AND INTEGRITY

THE SONG OF THE BOW

As David lamented the death of Saul and Jonathan, he composed a song he called "The Song of the Bow." Saul's death opened the door to the throne room for David, but David chose not to gloat over the fall of the mighty king. He had no desire to erase the memory of Saul for his own advantage. Rather, he created a song that would continue to remind his followers of their heritage. When he wrote the song, he directed that it be taught to the children of Judah.

David wanted Israel to know that Saul had been a great leader. He spoke of "the bow of Jonathan" and "the sword of Saul" as being effective in fighting Israel's battles. David was grateful for their contribution to the nation and celebrated their courage in battle. "Saul and Jonathan were beloved and pleasant in their lives, and in their death they were not divided; they were swifter than eagles, they were stronger than lions" (2 Samuel 1:23).

David wanted the nation to know they lived better lives because of Saul's reign. His passing was certainly a cause for national mourning. He urged the daughters of Israel, "O daughters of Israel, weep over Saul, who clothed you in scarlet with luxury; who put ornaments of gold on your apparel" (2 Samuel 1:24). He bore no jealousy toward the deceased king. Rather, David urged the people to recognize all that Saul had done, as he understood that it was only natural they would continue to love and honor the memory of their fallen king.

GREAT LEADERS REMEMBER THE VERY BEST OF THE VERY WORST

One expression of David's grief was articulated in a curse on Gilboa, the place of Saul's death. "O mountains of Gilboa, let there be no dew nor rain upon you, nor fields of offerings. For the shield of the mighty is cast away there! The shield of Saul, not anointed with oil" (2 Samuel 1:21). Visitors to Israel are shown the barren top of Mount Gilboa, while the mountains around are green. The curse on Gilboa remains even today.

While David mourned the loss of both Saul and Jonathan, his special relationship with Jonathan made his death particularly difficult to face. "I am distressed for you, my brother Jonathan; you have been pleasant to me; your love to me was wonderful, surpassing the love of women" (2 Samuel 1:26). He would grieve over the loss of a dear friend much longer than he would grieve over the king who had pursued him for so long.

KING OF JUDAH

In light of Saul's death, David once again turned to God for direction in his life. He knew he had a strong support base in Judah, but was unsure if the timing was right for him to assume the throne. God made it clear that he and his men should settle in Hebron, one of the cities that had shared in David's spoils. Once they confirmed that this plan was consistent with God's will, they moved into the city and surrounding villages.

Not long after he settled in Hebron, a delegation of elders from various cities in Judah arrived to meet with David. They had come to a consensus that David should lead their tribe as king. Although Samuel had anointed David in a private ceremony as Israel's next king, the men of Judah "anointed David king over the house of Judah" (2 Samuel 2:4). This highly symbolic act made his coronation official. They could only hope other tribes would soon see what they saw in David and make him king over all Israel.

As the oil flowed from his head and down his bearded face, David must have thought back to the day he had stood in the presence of Samuel. Much had transpired in the intervening years. A comparatively minor victory over a Philistine giant had catapulted David into the role of a national military hero. He had experienced the favor of King Saul and learned the inner workings of the palace. He had also experienced the king's wrath, forcing him into exile for fourteen long years. Yet even in those years, he had come to understand other cultures better and learned details he might not have otherwise learned about the nations that would soon be his enemies. There had been many dark hours and difficult days, but now the light at the end of the tunnel was finally coming into view. At last, it all was starting to make sense. God had his plan, and He was working all the things David had experienced for his good and God's glory.

GREAT LEADERS ARE PREPARED TO WAIT ON GOD'S TIMING

It was not until he had been anointed king of Judah that David learned of the heroic actions of the men of Jabesh Gilead. While the rest of Israel had been stunned into shock by the news of Saul's death, these men had rescued the bodies of Saul and his sons from public humiliation, brought them back to their own city, burned them so they could no longer be used by the enemy even if they were found, and buried them near their city by a prominent tree. When David heard of their deeds, he sent messengers to the city to commend them for their accomplishment.

Even as he grieved over the death of Saul and Jonathan, David understood the pain and grief felt by the city. He may have been concerned that they feared that he wanted to set the record straight and would perform a retaliatory act now that he was king of Judah. However, David had no intention of seeking revenge for past wrongs. It was time to move on as a unified nation. He only wanted the best for his people.

In his message to Jabesh Gilead, David made his views clear. "You are blessed of the LORD, for you have shown this kindness to your lord, to Saul, and have buried him. And now may the LORD show kindness and truth to you. I also will repay you this kindness, because you have done this thing. Now therefore, let your hands be strengthened, and be valiant; for your master Saul is dead, and also the house of Judah has anointed me king over them" (2 Samuel 2:5-7). He apparently hoped his sincere expression of empathy would help bring together factions of a divided and grieving nation.

GREAT LEADERS REACH OUT WITH EMPATHY TO THOSE WHO ARE HURTING

THE WAR HE TRIED TO AVOID

When a national leader dies suddenly, that nation always finds itself in a vulnerable position. This situation is complicated even more when there is no apparent strong leader to step into the leadership role. Had Saul died and Jonathan survived the battle against the Philistines, it is likely Jonathan would have quickly been accepted as king. In David's case, even though Samuel had anointed him years earlier, there were no guarantees that his right to rule would be widely recognized.

Despite his appeal to others to join Judah under his monarchy, there were many in Israel who felt the line of Saul could be carried on through Ishbosheth. Ishbosheth had not gone into battle with Saul and could claim the throne of his father by right of succession. Further, Ishbosheth had the support of Abner who commanded Saul's army. It was Abner who had been responsible for carrying out Saul's orders during David's years in exile, orders that included pursuing David since he was perceived as a threat to national security.

In light of David being anointed by Judah as their king, Abner moved fast to prevent the rest of the nation from following Judah's example. He quickly arranged a ceremony at Mahanaim where the other eleven tribes of Israel publicly recognized Ishbosheth as their king. As Judah remained committed to David's leadership, Abner's action divided the nation of Israel into two distinct nations. Ishbosheth ruled Israel and David ruled Judah.

Although forty years old, Ishbosheth had lived in the shadow of his father Saul and brother Jonathan so long that he had never really developed as a leader. Events that would transpire proved that he was inadequate for the task. In contrast, David was a now a strong and proven leader. Yet David remained concerned for the welfare of Israel and was opposed to armed conflict between brothers. For two years, the two kings were able to maintain peace between the two nations they ruled. Unfortunately, those responsible for each military were not as committed to peace as the kings they served.

Abner and Joab, Commander of Judah's army, agreed to meet in Gibeon, each apparently having an ulterior motive for their meeting. They may have met like this often to discuss issues of mutual defense. This time, as they gathered around the pool of Gibeon, each leader was looking for an opportunity to do harm to the other. It was Abner who initiated the action, but he quickly learned that Joab had come prepared to do the same.

When allies met together, it was customary to conduct war games so each could demonstrate their strength on the battlefield. Normally, the fighting was intense but not fatal. On this occasion, Abner had instructed his men to kill the men they fought, knowing this action would ignite a civil war. He assumed his betrayal of trust would catch Joab off guard and he would be able to destroy the leadership of Judah's army. If he was successful, it would only be a matter of time before he could defeat the rest of Judah's army and unify the nation under Ishbosheth.

This game called for a dozen men to compete on each side. As soon as the action began, Abner's men thrust their swords into their opponent's side. What Abner did not realize was that Joab had given his men similar orders. Within moments, twenty-four soldiers lay dead on the ground. A fierce conflict arose immediately and continued throughout the day. Although Abner had counted on the element of surprise to give him the upper hand, he was soon on the losing end of the battle.

Before the battle concluded, Israel's army scattered and was pursued by Judah's army. Joab's brother Asahel spotted Abner in the distance and began pursuing the one who had begun this conflict. Asahel's speed as a runner was legendary in Judah, often compared to the speed of a gazelle. It was not long before Asahel closed in on Abner. Joab and his other brother Abishai were also in pursuit of Abner, but they were still a long distance away from him.

Abner had a lot of respect for Asahel and had hoped they

would serve together in a unified army under Ishbosheth. When he realized Asahel was pursuing him, he urged him to turn aside and let him escape. When Asahel kept pursuing him, he warned him he would have to defend himself if he continued in the pursuit. Still Asahel gained ground and came closer. Finally, apparently in an attempt to wind Asahel so he would not be able to continue running after him, "Abner struck him in the stomach with the blunt end of the spear, so that the spear came out his back; and he fell down there and died on the spot" (2 Samuel 2:23).

As the sun began going down over the mountains near Gibeon, Abner called out to Joab for a truce and an end to the day's fighting. Joab agreed and the two armies returned to their capitals. The battle had cost Judah twenty men including Asahel. Yet the cost for Israel's army was three hundred and sixty men. Beyond that, the death of Asahel created a feud between the leader of each army, which would complicate efforts to peacefully resolve the conflict.

This was a situation David had attempted to avoid at all costs, but now that war had been declared, he had no choice but to engage in the fight. He would unify the nation through conflict if he could not do it through peaceful negotiations. "Now there was a long war between the house of Saul and the house of David" (2 Samuel 3:1).

GREAT LEADERS DO WHAT NEEDS TO BE DONE, EVEN WHEN THEY WOULD RATHER NOT

CHAPTER SEVEN

WHEN YOU BLOW IT WITH THE BEST OF INTENTIONS

2 Samuel 5:1-6:23; 1 Chronicles 11:1-9; 13:1-16:43

At times, the long wait must have seemed like it would go on forever. When the tribe of Judah made him their king, David must have realized Samuel's vision for his life was finally coming to pass. He would indeed be king over all Israel. But here he was, having lived half his life and it seemed he was no closer to unifying the kingdom under his rule than he had been during those many years in the wilderness being hunted down by Saul. At least Saul had done something he had not yet been able to do. He ruled a united nation. David, it appeared, had been the cause for dividing that nation.

When voters express their frustration with the governing party by electing an opposing party to office, the transition from being the opposition to ruling as government is often difficult to make. When Judah invited David to be their king, he entered into a transition period in his own life. It was one thing to fight Israel's enemies as the leader of a mercenary force that was living in exile. It was something quite different to oppose them as a king. Though the seven and a half years ruling as king of Judah may have been frustrating at times, this time period gave him time to build his credibility. Judah had time to confirm they had made the right choice in a king. Israel had time to realize that David had what it took to be king. The nations surrounding Israel and Judah had time to realize that David would be a force to be reckoned with in the days to come.

Sometimes, God's apparent delays are being used for a larger purpose. This may explain some of what took place as David waited to rule a united nation. Israel was a strong nation, and in their strength they had chosen to follow a weak king. Israel's king, Ishbosheth, was apparently born after Saul had turned from God and begun worshipping Baal. Elsewhere in Scripture he is called Esh-Baal, which means "man of Baal" (1 Chronicles 8:33; 9:39). His name Ishbosheth means "man of shame." During the civil war between Judah and the other tribes of Israel, "David grew stronger and stronger, and the house of Saul grew weaker and weaker" (2 Samuel 3:1). During that time, Ishbosheth became an embarrassment to his nation. Perhaps God delayed apparent progress in David's life because the people of Israel had to become weak enough to want a strong king.

Israel was not the only one who needed time to prepare to accept David as king. Initially, Abner was the driving force in convincing Israel to make Ishbosheth their king rather than David (2 Samuel 2:8, 9). As a commander in Saul's army, he likely acted out of a deep sense of personal loyalty to his fallen king. He may have realized that Ishbosheth lacked the leadership skills needed to rule a nation, but capable men who would be part of the royal court could compensate for his weakness. Unfortunately, the longer Abner served under the king he had supported, the more obvious it was, even to him, that he had made a grave mistake.

The matter came to a head when Abner began a relationship with one of Saul's former concubines, a woman named Rizpah. At that time, it was customary for a conquering king to bring the wives and concubines of the former king into his harem. Ishbosheth, an insecure leader despite his title, saw Abner's action as a threat against his throne. Overlooking years of loyal service, he chose to confront his general over the matter. "Why have you gone in to my father's concubine?" he asked (2 Samuel 3:7).

Ishbosheth's statement was more than a question. It was an accusation of high treason. Years of frustration over Ishbosheth's failure to develop as a leader caused Abner to respond indignantly to the ridiculous charge. Did he not realize he was only on the throne because of Abner's continued loyalty? Is this the way a king rewards a loyal servant? "Today I show loyalty to the house of Saul your father, to his brothers, and to his friends, and have not delivered you into the hand of David; and you charge me today with a fault concerning this woman?" (2 Samuel 3:8). A man to whom he pledged his loyalty was treating him worse than a dog. The King's accusation pushed Abner over the edge. If Ishbosheth wanted to accuse him of acting out treason, then that's exactly what he would do.

"May God do so to Abner, and more also, if I do not do for David as the LORD has sworn to him – to transfer the kingdom from the house of Saul, and set up the throne of David over Israel and over Judah, from Dan to Beersheba" (2 Samuel 3:9, 10). Abner had become frustrated enough to want a faithful king. He would no longer resist God's will for the nation. He knew God had promised the throne to David. By now everyone in Israel knew. Abner also knew he was strong enough to make it happen, and in time he would!

GREAT LEADERS ALLOW THEIR PEOPLE TIME TO CHANGE

ONE NATION – ONE KING

Abner had little difficulty convincing Israel to embrace David as their new king. For seven and a half years, Israel had been a fractured family, incomplete without the tribe of Judah. The nation knew Judah was the tribe from which Israel's kings would rise. Jacob himself had declared, "The scepter shall not depart from Judah, nor a lawgiver from between his feet, until Shiloh comes" (Genesis 49:10). When it came time to unite the nation, Israel was prepared to confess, "Indeed we are your bone and your flesh" (2 Samuel 5:1).

Not only was David from the right tribe, he had proved himself as a capable leader. His track record spoke for itself. "In time past, when Saul was king over us, you were the one who led Israel out and brought them in" (2 Samuel 5:2). Saul may have held the title, but the people recognized that it was David who was doing the work of a king. That recognition had irritated Saul so much that he caused David to live in exile for thirteen years. Now, the source of David's problems served as a foundation for his ministry.

In the New Testament, Paul explained this principle to the Corinthians. God sometimes allows problems to come into a Christian's life simply for the purpose of equipping them to be more effective in ministry to others. "Blessed be the God and Father of our Lord Jesus Christ, the Father of mercies and God of all comfort, who comforts us in all our tribulation, that we may be able to comfort those who are in any trouble, with the comfort with which we ourselves are comforted by God" (2 Corinthians 1:3, 4).

The nation of Israel also recognized God's call upon David's life to be their king. They understood that God had promised David, "You shall shepherd My people Israel, and be ruler over Israel" (2 Samuel 5:2). By the time Israel came to anoint David as their king, they were a hurting nation. The long civil war had weakened their economy and national resolve. Several key leaders among them had been victims of violence. They needed a king with compassion. If David would "shepherd" them as a nation, they would make him their ruler.

David had already taken action to demonstrate that he was such a king. When Joab killed Abner out of revenge for Asahel's death, the king publicly mourned at Abner's grave. Even when his rival Ishbosheth was murdered, David refused to reward those who had killed their king. Rather he ordered them executed for killing "a righteous person in his own house on his bed" (2 Samuel 4:11). Israel saw in David a man who did not hold grudges but was willing to embrace former enemies. "Therefore all the elders of Israel came to the king at Hebron, and King David made a covenant with them at Hebron before the LORD. And they anointed David king over Israel" (2 Samuel 5:3).

GREAT LEADERS EARN THE TRUST OF THOSE WHO FOLLOW THEM

With the unification of the nation under a single king accomplished, David realized he needed to strengthen the nation's unity by embracing the eleven tribes as equal partners with Judah. For seven and a half years, he had ruled Judah from Hebron, one of the principle cities belonging to that tribe. He could have moved his capital to a city belonging to one of the other tribes, but to do so would alienate Judah. Instead, he came up with another plan.

Jerusalem was uniquely situated along the boundary between Judah and Benjamin; although Israel had now possessed the land for about four centuries, the city had never been conquered. That meant the city belonged to neither Judah nor Benjamin. This made Jerusalem an ideal choice for a capital. If he conquered the city, it would thereafter be known as "the city of David" in the minds of all Israel rather than associated with any one tribe. Also, the unique geology of the area made Jerusalem a very defendable capital, an important consideration with so many enemies living nearby. Ultimately, it was David's intention to make Jerusalem the center of worship in Israel, the place Moses had described in the law (Deuteronomy 12:5). That act would forever elevate Jerusalem as "the city of God."

GREAT LEADERS UNDERSTAND THE SIGNIFICANCE OF GREAT SYMBOLS

ACCOMPLISHING THE IMPOSSIBLE

There was something about Jerusalem that seemed to fascinate

David. As he shepherded his father's flocks in Bethlehem to the south, he had often seen the city set on the hill to the north. The Jebusites who inhabited the city had lived in relative peace with Israel since the nation first entered the land under Joshua's leadership. David likely had accompanied his father to the city on occasion, especially if Jesse's business with the Jebusites included buying or selling sheep. Although David came from a prominent family in Bethlehem, Jerusalem was the kind of city he surely admired.

Even if he had not been to the city with his father, other events in David's earlier life required him to pass by the city. The road passed by Jerusalem as he traveled from Bethlehem to Gibeah, which had been Saul's capital. That was the road he would have traveled on his way to Saul's palace when he was called upon to serve as court musician. He would have passed by Jerusalem again on his way to take supplies to his brothers fighting in Saul's army in the valley of Elah. In fact, David had made a point of visiting Jerusalem the day he conquered Goliath (1 Samuel 17:54). Perhaps he had already decided then that Jerusalem would someday be his capital.

Making Jerusalem his capital would not be an easy task. The very reasons Jerusalem would make an excellent capital city were the greatest obstacles to making it so. The city's founders had built their city on a high plateau. While that made the city visible, it also meant the watchmen of the city could see armies advancing miles away. Even then, they really didn't need the advanced warning. The city was surrounded on three sides by steep valleys that were difficult to scale. The fourth side of the city provided a natural rocky defense against attack. It was widely believed the city was impregnable. Four centuries of history only reinforced that assumption.

The Jebusites were so confident they could not be defeated, they laughed when they learned of David's ambition. "You shall not come in here; but the blind and the lame will repel you," they boasted (2 Samuel 5:6). They knew David and his army would fail in any attempt to take the city. Unfortunately, there were probably too many in David's army who shared this sentiment. But David did not. He clearly heard the words the Jebusites called out to him. Soon he would use those very words to motivate his own troops in battle. David was still willing to dream the impossible dream.

GREAT LEADERS DREAM BEYOND THEIR LIMITS

David would change fear to confidence by giving his men a bite-sized taste of victory. Like any other great military leader, he clearly identified his objectives in the upcoming battle. His motto was simple and easy to remember. "Defeat the Jebusites" (1 Samuel 5:8). David would require this accomplishment alone of his soldiers in this battle. When the Jebusites were defeated, Israel's soldiers would know they had achieved victory.

But dreaming great dreams and talking about them was not enough. David knew he needed a viable strategy to conquer the city. The usual practices of battle would not work at Jerusalem. Too many soldiers would die in a frontal assault and there was no guarantee victory would be theirs in the end. He didn't have time for a siege. The city might hold out for years and he needed a quick victory now. There had to be another way to take the city, a way no army in the last four hundred years had considered.

David knew a way into the city even the Jebusites had overlooked. That knowledge would be the key to his battle plan. In his novel, *David: Warrior and King*, Frank Slaughter suggests that David discovered the passage when he dunked his head in a pool and heard noises he concluded came from the city. Slaughter postulates that further investigation led to the discovery of the soft underbelly of the city.[1] Perhaps this is how David discovered the water tunnel, a secret entrance into the city. Many Bible teachers believe David discovered it years earlier exploring the area as a young shepherd.

David proposed that a small force could scale the cavern and enter the city covertly while the rest of the army remained encamped below. The Jebusites would be so preoccupied with the army in the valley below they would not consider an invasion from the heart of the city. Four hundred years of security probably meant those responsible for defending the city had little experience, if any, in battle. They would be no match for David's soldiers, soldiers who had experienced many battles in the civil war that had just ended.

While David knew his army could defeat the Jebusites, some soldiers apparently needed further encouragement. Now was the time to use the Jebusites own claim against them. David's army had heard the same words David had heard as the city's residents had called down to mock them. Who did they think they were anyway? "The lame and the blind, who are hated by David's soul" (2 Samuel 5:8). As David used that language to describe the enemy, throughout the camp of Israel men began believing that David's dream may not be so impossible after all. What kind of soldiers would they be if they could not conquer a city of "the lame and the blind?"

Now all David needed was a capable leader to command the invasion force. He would make it worthwhile to accept such a risk. "Whoever attacks the Jebusites first shall be chief and captain," he promised (1 Chronicles 11:6). David had decided that, as king, he would surround himself with the kind of men who knew how to get the job done. There were many theorists willing to give advice in Israel, but their advice was unproven. When he looked to others for advice, David would listen to those who knew what worked due to their experience.

David's cousin Joab quickly rose to the challenge. Perhaps under cover of darkness, Joab quietly took a band of soldiers to the secret cave. They probably had to crawl over each other, forming a human ladder, to scale the entrance of the cave. Once the first man entered the crevice that led to the heart of the city, others could scale the rock using a rope. As soon as they crawled out of the cavern and entered the city, they began the work they were sent to do. The battle was not long. When they had done their job, they opened the city gates to let the rest of the army in. The city of the Jebusites was now the city of David.

GREAT LEADERS FIND WAYS TO MAKE THINGS HAPPEN

Jerusalem was unique among all the cities of Israel in that there were no "blue bloods" and "newcomers" living within the city walls. Every citizen of Jerusalem was a stranger and made the city their home regardless of tribal background. No doubt every tribe now had citizens serving their king as advisors or part of the royal guard. In that sense, the city belonged to everyone and became a symbol that, regardless of their tribal background, they were now part of a single nation. David understood they were, in a very special way, "one nation under God." The key to communicating this to the rest of the nation was to make the city the center of worship for all Israel.

DISTRACTED BY SUCCESS

Years earlier, Moses had insisted to Israel, at God's command, that they not be like other nations in their worship. His vision for the nation He had brought out of Egypt involved centralized worship. The Canaanites established their worship centers wherever there was a high hill or large oak. They were scattered throughout the land. "But you shall seek the place where the LORD your God chooses, out of all your tribes, to put His name for His dwelling place; and there shall you go," Moses urged (Deuteronomy 12:5). Deep in his heart, David knew that place was Jerusalem...the ancient city where their Father Abraham was first introduced to God by name. (See Genesis 14:18-22)

If Jerusalem was to be the worship center of Israel, his next great task would be to bring the Ark of the Covenant to his new capital. The Ark of the Covenant was part of the original furnishings of the tabernacle. By divine design, it was the only thing that remained in the holiest part of the worship tent. It held Israel's most sacred treasures: the Ten Commandments carved in stone by the hand of God, Aaron's rod that had budded in the wilderness, and a jar of manna collected in the wilderness to remind Israel of God's provision for forty years. But as special as the contents of the ark were, it was the lid of ark that held special significance for David and all Israel. It was there, between the wings of the cherubim, that God had promised to meet the High Priest, the nation's representative before God.

David's ambition to move the ark to Jerusalem was not wrong. He appealed to the national assembly, "Let us bring the ark of our God back to us, for we have not inquired at it since the days of Saul" (1 Chronicles 13:3). It had been used little during Saul's reign and not at all since. His motive was commendable. David wanted to restore the ark to its rightful place in the worship of Israel. He knew even the act of bringing the ark to Jerusalem would be cause for a great celebration and worship of God (1 Chronicles 13:8). There can be little doubt the king launched this endeavor with the best of intentions.

He proposed that the ark be carried to the city on a new cart pulled by oxen. While no one objected to the plan, David should have known better. His early psalms reflect a deep devotion not only to God but also the Scriptures. As a student of the Scriptures, he knew God had prescribed a specific way to transport the ark from place to place. "You shall put the poles into the rings on the sides of the ark, that the ark may be carried by them" (Exodus 25:15). Later, he would remind the Levites of their responsibility in moving the ark from place to place, suggesting they were responsible for the tragedy about to befall the nation (1 Chronicles 15:13). But as he proposed his initial plan, the king seemed to be distracted from doing the right thing the right way.

Sometimes, the most dangerous times in a leader's tenure of service are his moments of success. David had waited a long time to be king of all Israel, more than twenty years. Now suddenly it seemed like he could do nothing wrong. Israel had been united by diplomacy, not victory. It was better than he could have hoped for throughout the long civil war. He had chosen to attack a city that had been undefeated for four centuries, and won. Could it be that in the rush of success, David had come to believe he was no longer dependent upon the One who had been his Strength throughout the past two decades?

GREAT LEADERS ALWAYS REMEMBER WHAT MADE THEM GREAT IN THE FIRST PLACE

Precedents that have been set have a power that often hinders leaders as they seek to lead in new and creative ways. Precedents are not always bad as they can bring stability to weak institutions. But they can also stifle creativity in strong institutions. Precedents may exert more power than they should in an organization when leaders begin hearing statements like, "We've always done it that way" and "If it's not broken, why fix it?"

Israel had not always moved the ark on a cart, but there was a precedent for doing so. This was the means used by the Philistines when they chose to transport the ark back to Israel (1 Samuel 6:3-8). Even though their actions violated the principles laid down by Moses, things seemed to work well for them. Actually, the Philistine plan resulted in God lifting the plague from them that had been His judgment for taking the ark in the first place. No doubt there were those in Israel who reasoned, "If it worked for the Philistines, it should work for us." David may have been among them.

Leaders are also sometimes distracted by polls. While it may be a popular strategy with the politicians and the people who elect them to office, it is not good leadership. A leader who follows his people is not leading them.

It is interesting to notice how David began his address to the national assembly as he outlined his plan for moving the ark. "If it seems good to you…" Could it be that this leader of men was on the verge of converting from statesman to politician? It sounded like it. "Then all the assembly said that they would do so, for the thing was right in the eyes of all the people" (1 Chronicles 13:4). At this point it is easy to wonder if David would have pursued his plan if it had proved unpopular with the assembly. Sometimes, a leader knows what is best for the people regardless of what the crowd thinks. Did David simply propose a plan that he knew the people would endorse?

David took what he thought were the necessary precautions to implement his plan. He placed two sons of Abinadab in charge of the actual moving of the ark. The family of Abinadab had cared for the ark during the years of neglect. It was doubtful that there was anyone else left in Israel that had any practical experience with this treasured religious symbol. In accordance with David's plan, a new cart had been constructed for the journey to Jerusalem and the yoke was fitted to the ox. The sons of Abinadab probably moved the ark from their home to the cart in accordance with the principles laid down by Moses.

As the project unfolded, there was cause for great celebration. "Then David and all Israel played music before God with all their might, with singing, on harps, on stringed instruments, on tambourines, on cymbals, and with trumpets" (1 Chronicles 13:8). It had been a long time since such worship had been experienced in Israel. Those present no doubt felt they were witnessing something they would never forget. They had no idea just how memorable the day would be.

Everything was going according to plan until "they came to Chidon's threshing floor" (1 Chronicles 13:9). The oxen, used to the feel of the earth beneath their feet, began to slip and stumble as they stepped onto the smoother surface of the threshing floor. The twist in the oxen's yoke caused the wagon to tilt to one side slightly and for a moment it appeared the ark itself might slide off the cart and be damaged as it fell to the earth. That's when Uzzah stepped forward to save the day. He reached out to grab the ark and prevent it from falling and being damaged. But as his hand came in contact with Israel's sacred treasure, "the anger of the LORD was aroused against Uzzah, and He struck him because he put his hand to the ark; and he died there before God" (1 Chronicles 13:10).

Touching the ark for any reason was forbidden in the law of God. The furnishings of the tabernacle had been designed with rings so they could be carried with poles. When first given the responsibility of transporting the furnishings of the tabernacle, the Levites were warned not to "touch any holy thing, lest they die" (Numbers 4:15). Regardless of the reason, the law of God had been violated and the promised severe judgment had been inflicted.

David was furious. How could this happen to him? Didn't God understand what he was doing? How could something that felt so right moments ago end up so wrong? Few in Israel had ever seen him so angry before. It was a sight they would not soon forget. They would always remember that place as Perez Uzzah, Master of Breakthroughs (1 Chronicles 13:11).

But deep down, David already knew the answers to his questions. It was not God who was wrong in this action but Israel's new king. Perhaps he had known all along there was a better way to move the ark – God's way. He had chosen his own agenda over that which God had established. How did that make him any different from Saul, his predecessor? In light of what he had just witnessed, how might he expect God to deal with him if he continued this project? As quickly as his anger had erupted, it changed to fear. No matter how popular the project had been, it was too dangerous to go on. The journey ended there and the ark was moved into the home of Obed-Edom the Gittite (1 Chronicles 13:13).

GREAT LEADERS KNOW THE TASTE OF FAILURE

The king returned to his capital where there was much to do to take his mind off the tragedy he had witnessed, the tragedy he had caused. Still, it was not long before the fear that caused him to abandon the project changed into a frustration that the ark was still not in Jerusalem. This frustration only increased as he heard how "the LORD blessed the house of Obed-Edom and all he had" (1 Chronicles 13:14). Had David accomplished his original goal, that blessing would belong to him and his city. Three months after the project had been abandoned, the king made a decision. He would again try to transport the ark to Jerusalem, but this time he had a different plan.

FAILING FORWARD TO ACCOMPLISH THE GOAL

David's first step in the new plan to bring the ark to Jerusalem took place in the royal city itself. "He prepared a place for the ark of God, and pitched a tent for it" (1 Chronicles 15:1). Some Bible teachers believe that David had moved the tabernacle to Jerusalem prior to the previous attempt to move the ark, but there is no specific mention of that action in the biblical text. He may have planned to place the ark on public display in the capital previously, but this time he prepared the kind of place Moses had prepared to properly house the ark. This new tent in Jerusalem eventually became known as "the Tabernacle of David" (Amos 9:11; Acts 15:16).

Next he determined they would no longer be using a cart. The Philistine precedent would be replaced by an earlier pattern established by Moses. It was not open to discussion this time. Regardless of what others might think, David simply declared, "No one may carry the ark of God but the Levites for the LORD has chosen them to carry the ark of God and to minister before Him forever" (1 Chronicles 15:2).

David called the priests and Levites together to organize them to accomplish the task (1 Chronicles 15:3-10). Addressing the heads of their households, he challenged them to "bring up the ark of the LORD God of Israel to the place I have prepared for it" (1 Chronicles 15:12). It seemed like a simple task, but perhaps that is where things had gone wrong in the previous attempt.

David felt it was important the Levites understood the solemnity of the task they were being charged to carry out. "For because you did not do it the first time, the LORD our God broke out against us, because we did not consult Him about the proper order" (1 Chronicles 15:13). David had learned his lesson. He could only hope the Levites had learned the same lesson.

GREAT LEADERS LEARN FROM THEIR MISTAKES AND ADJUST THEIR LIVES ACCORDINGLY

Finally the day came for implementing the new plan to transport the Ark of the Covenant to Jerusalem. "So the priests and the Levites sanctified themselves to bring up the ark of the LORD God of Israel. And the children of the Levites bore the ark of God on their shoulders, by its poles, as Moses had commanded according to the word of the LORD" (1 Chronicles 15:14, 15). David watched as the Levites took that first step, then another. "And so it was, when those bearing the ark of the LORD had gone six paces, that he sacrificed oxen and fatted sheep" (2 Samuel 6:13).

The text is not clear as to whether David's sacrifices were a one-time event on the journey or whether it was repeated every six paces. Kings often made an abundance of sacrifices and many commentators believe David must have repeated this procedure often on the journey to Bethlehem. It would have been quite a spectacle to see the route dotted with priests and Levites offering sacrifices to God.

This time, there truly was cause for celebration. "Then David danced before the LORD with all his might; and David was wearing a linen ephod. So David and all the house of Israel brought up the ark the LORD with shouting and with the sound of the trumpet" (2 Samuel 6:14, 15). The king and his people were lost in reckless abandonment as they worshipped their God. When the ark was set in its place, "then David offered burnt offerings and peace offerings before the LORD" (2 Samuel 6:17). In Israel's worship, the burnt offering was an expression of total dedication to God. The peace offering was used to celebrate the restoration of a fractured relationship. Having successfully brought the ark to Jerusalem, David expressed his total commitment to his relationship with God in the most public manner possible.

This was indeed a day of celebration. There was no reason why anyone in the city should not be a part of the festivities. The king appeared before those gathered and "blessed the people in the name of the LORD of hosts. Then he distributed among all the people, among the whole multitude of Israel, both the women and the men, to everyone a loaf of bread, a piece of meat, and a cake of raisins" (2 Samuel 6:19). He would send them home to celebrate with their families, but there was one thing more to do.

This was also a day that should not ever be forgotten. The chronicler of Judah records, "On that day David first delivered this psalm into the hand of Asaph and his brethren, to thank the LORD" (1 Chronicles 16:7). David knew people had a tendency to forget great events they experience. He also knew music had the power to bring back memories. Every time his people heard this song, they would remember the very first time they heard it. This would be "their song." And to ensure that they would hear it often, he incorporated the song recorded in 1 Chronicles 16:8-36 into at least three other songs that Israel would sing often as they gathered together to worship (Psalms 96:3-9; 105:1-15; 106:47, 48).

GREAT LEADERS
HELP THEIR PEOPLE REMEMBER
GREAT ACCOMPLISHMENTS

CHAPTER EIGHT

WHEN THE THING YOU WANTED MOST IN LIFE IS NOT GOING TO HAPPEN

2 Samuel 7:1-29; 1 Chronicles 17:1-27; 22:1-29:20

After years of struggle, it seemed David could finally relax and do the things he really wanted to do. He was only sixteen years old when the prophet Samuel had poured the anointing oil over his head to announce he would be Israel's next king. A year later, he defeated Goliath in the Valley of Elah, an act that catapulted him into prominence as a leader in Saul's army. In spite of his success and what he knew to be the promise of God, David remained loyal to Saul as he led troops into battle. David's continued success in battle unfortunately stirred a deep jealousy and resentment in King Saul toward his successor.

For thirteen years, Saul pursued David through the wilderness. Throughout those years, he held tightly to the promise of God concerning his destiny. Finally, at age thirty, David began to see that dream realized as the elders of Judah designated him as their new king. He had hoped the other tribes of Israel would quickly support his claim to the throne, but that would only happen after a bloody seven-year civil war.

When the war concluded with the unification of the nation,

there were still more battles to be fought. He chose the unconquered city of Jerusalem to be his capital and drove the Jebusites
from their stronghold, something that had not been done in over
four hundred years. There in the new "City of David" he built his
palace made from the finest cedars of Lebanon. Wanting his capital to be more than a political center, he finally moved the Ark of
the Covenant to Jerusalem, making it the worship center of the
nation.

David already had accomplished more than he dreamed possible and was enjoying the fruits of his labors. He had conquered
those who posed a threat to his nation. Political observers of the
day might have concluded that all was well in the kingdom, as it
certainly appeared that way. Still, one thing seemed out of place to
David.

THE ULTIMATE PROJECT FOR A KING

"Now it came to pass when the king was dwelling in his house,
and the LORD had given him rest from all his enemies all
around, that the king said to Nathan the prophet, "See now, I
dwell in a house of cedar, but the ark of God dwells inside tent
curtains" (2 Samuel 7:1, 2). David struggled with his comfortable lifestyle compared to the condition of the Tabernacle which
had served Israel for centuries.

Throughout his life, David had a deep and abiding passion for
God. This love for God naturally expressed itself in a desire to
worship God. Many of the psalms he wrote would be used by
Israel, and later the Christian churches, to express praise and worship to God. Because the worship of God was centralized in the
Tabernacle, it was only natural that David continually longed to
worship God in that setting.

The thought of worshipping God freely in the Tabernacle was
one of the things that gave David hope during his long years of
wandering and being pursued by Saul. "One thing I have desired
of the LORD, that will I seek: that I may dwell in the house of the
LORD all the days of my life, to behold the beauty of the LORD,

and to inquire in His temple" (Psalm 27:4). David was convinced there was a relationship between the time spent in worship and communion with God and God's protection and promotion in his life. "For in the time of trouble He shall hide me in His pavilion; in the secret place of His tabernacle He shall hide me; He shall set me high upon a rock" (Psalm 27:4).

It just did not seem right to David that he lived in a comfortable palace and that a decaying tent remained the national symbol of the worship of God. He longed to build another palace, greater than his own. This would be a palace for the worship of God. Even the structure itself would remind all who came to worship of the awesomeness of their God. As he described his vision to Nathan, he learned he was not alone in his opinion. "Then Nathan said to the king, 'Go, do all that is in your heart, for the LORD is with you'" (2 Samuel 7:3).

GREAT LEADERS SERVE A PURPOSE GREATER THAN THEMSELVES

WHEN GOD SAYS "NO!"

As David laid his head on the pillow that night, after speaking with Nathan, he may have had a difficult time getting to sleep. The thing David wanted to do more than anything else in the world was finally going to happen. He would build a temple worthy of the God who had done so much for him. His mind surely raced as he considered various aspects of the project and what the finished building might look like. It would have to be greater than any temple he had ever seen that was devoted to the gods of other nations.

David understood that God dwelt among His people in a special way in the Ark of the Covenant. When Israel was in the wilderness, the ark rested in the holiest place in the Tabernacle and both were moved as Israel moved. But Israel was now settled in her own land and there was no need to keep the ark in a mobile worship center.

Just as the people now lived in their own comfortable homes, the time had come for the ark to have its own home in Jerusalem.

But David was not the only one who had difficulty sleeping that night. Although Nathan had agreed that David's idea was good and told him to proceed, God had other plans. That evening, Nathan heard from God and was given a difficult assignment. "Go and tell my servant David. 'Thus says the LORD: "Would you build a house for Me to dwell in? For I have not dwelt in a house since the time that I brought the children of Israel up from Egypt, even to this day, but have moved about in a tent and in a tabernacle" (2 Samuel 7:5, 6).

God told Nathan to remind David of the blessings He had given to David. God had a plan for David, but it did not include building a temple. That task would be reserved for David's son and successor. As the sun broke over the mountains of Israel, Nathan made his way to the palace once again to reverse his previous day's advice.

GREAT LEADERS SOMETIMES FACE GREAT DISAPPOINTMENTS

WHEN GOD SAYS "NO!"
1. Look for a bigger goal, not a smaller one.
2. Look for a supernatural goal, not one you can do.
3. Look for an eternal goal, not one that will decay.
4. Look for a spiritual goal, not one of human origin.
5. Make Christ the focus of your goal.

BUILDING THE HOUSE OF DAVID

David listened to Nathan as he delivered his message from God. Although he was now king of a very powerful nation, he was reminded of his humble beginnings. "I took you from the sheep-fold, from following the sheep, to be ruler over My people Israel" (2 Samuel 7:8). God also reminded David that He was the reason for his success in life. "And I have been with you wherever you have gone, and have cut off all your enemies from before you, and have made you a great name, like the name of the great men who are on the earth" (2 Samuel 7:9). As David listened, he was reminded of why he wanted to build a temple for God.

Nathan continued to explain that God was indeed bringing Israel into a more settled lifestyle in which there would no longer be a need for a tabernacle, as opposed to a temple. The real problem was not in David's idea but his timing. The temple would be built, but not during David's reign. It would be built during the reign of his son. As for David, God had a better idea.

David wanted to build a temporary house for God, but God wanted to build an eternal house for David. Of the various worship centers used by Israel, the temple built by Solomon was probably the most elaborate, but it actually served Israel for a shorter time than either the Tabernacle or the new Temple built by the Jewish remnant following the Babylonian captivity. God instead offered David an unconditional covenant establishing his dynasty forever. The Davidic covenant is the basis of the Lord Jesus Christ's rule over all Israel during the coming millennial kingdom.

Under the terms of this covenant, God offered David several things. First, the line of David was guaranteed. He would have a member of his family alive for generations to come. Second, he and his descendants were also guaranteed a throne, the symbol of regal authority. Further, they would be kings with a kingdom, a sphere of influence over which they ruled. Fourth, this covenant, like other covenants God established throughout the Old Testament, would be unconditional. Finally, this covenant would be eternal, an unending covenant lasting forever. Based on this covenant, years later an angel would appear to a virgin in Galilee and announce, "Behold, you will conceive in your womb and bring forth a Son, and shall call His name Jesus. He will be great, and will be called the Son of the Highest; and the Lord God will give Him the throne of His father David, and He will reign over the house of Jacob forever, and of His kingdom there will be no end" (Luke 1:31-33).

The early chapters of the Bible describe several covenants God had previously established and honored, beginning with the original Edenic covenant before sin was a part of human experience. When that covenant was violated, subsequent covenants were made with Adam, Noah, and Abraham. God had established the last covenant of this nature when Israel left Egypt and worshipped Him at Mount Sinai. Although David had no way of knowing it, the only remaining covenant God would make would be the "New Covenant" promised to Ezekiel and Jeremiah as the nation was taken into captivity. What he did know was that this kind of offer did not come often. It was more than he probably had ever dreamed might happen.

GREAT LEADERS LET GOD CONTINUALLY STRETCH THEIR VISION

DAVID'S RESPONSE TO HIS KING

Overwhelmed with what he had learned, David made his way to the Tabernacle and marveled in awe of the God who had chosen to meet His people in that place. As he sat taking in all he had heard and began to understand something of what it meant, he soon started responding to God in prayer. The nations of the world might have viewed David as Israel's sovereign, but at moments like this, David knew who Israel's real King was. Knowing this gave him a more realistic perspective on who he really was.

Throughout David's prayer, he uses the title for God translated "Lord GOD." The name translated "Lord" is the Hebrew word Adonai which literally means "Master." The name translated "GOD" is the Hebrew word Jehovah which throughout Scripture is used to emphasize God's relationship with people. When used alone, it is usually translated "LORD" emphasizing God's sovereignty over His people. As David addresses God in this prayer, he recognizes that he is accountable to his Master and Lord, as any employee is accountable to his supervisor and boss.

This experience brought David to the point where he recognized his personal limitations. As much as he wanted to build the temple for God, he had been a man of war. God's purpose for him included conquering Israel's enemies and establishing the kingdom. As he sat before God in the tabernacle, he began praying, "Who am I, O Lord GOD? And what is my house, that You have brought me this far?" (2 Samuel 7:18). Even before he addressed the promises God was making, he expressed his sense of unworthiness for the blessings he had already received from God.

For years, even before he sat on the throne of Judah or Israel, David had been perceived as a champion of Israel. It had all begun that day in the Valley of Elah when he defeated Goliath. His success on the battlefield had become legendary in Israel and beyond. But sitting in the Tabernacle, his accomplishments seemed so small. "And yet this was a small thing in Your sight, O Lord GOD; and You have also spoken of your servant's house for a great while to come. Is this the manner of man of man, O Lord GOD? Now what more can David say to You? For You, Lord GOD, know Your servant" (2 Samuel 7:19, 20).

GREAT LEADERS ALWAYS KEEP THEIR HUMBLE STATUS IN PERSPECTIVE

As he continued praying, David acknowledged that all his past success was the result of God's goodness extended toward him. "For Your word's sake, and according to Your own heart, You have done all these great things, to make Your servant know them" (2 Samuel 7:21). He knew there was nothing in himself that warranted God's goodness. The decision to bless him had been made according to

God's sovereign grace.

Through his prior experience with God, David had learned much about who God is and how He relates to His people. "Therefore You are great, O Lord GOD. For there is none like You, nor is there any God besides You, according to all that we have heard with our ears. And who is like Your people, like Israel, the one nation on the earth whom God went to redeem for Himself as a people, to make for Himself a name – and to do for Yourself great and awesome deeds for Your land – before Your people whom You redeemed for Yourself from Egypt, the nations, and their gods? For You have made Your people Israel Your very own people forever; and You, LORD, have become their God" (2 Samuel 7:22-24).

God's message to David had been about the future. David's response to God included thanksgiving for the past. As Israel's king, he appreciated the unique heritage that belonged to the nation he ruled. He found it easy to believe what God said about the future because of the record of God's faithfulness in the past.

GREAT LEADERS REMEMBER THEIR GREAT HERITAGE

"Now, O LORD God, the word which You have spoken concerning Your servant and concerning his house, establish it for ever and do as You have said" (2 Samuel 7:25). In this portion of his prayer, David used God's Hebrew name Jehovah Elohim rather than the name Adonai Jehovah used predominately throughout the rest of the prayer. The name Jehovah is common to both compound names of God and emphasizes His covenant relationship with His people. The name Elohim is sometimes called "the creative name of God" because it is the first name of God found in Scripture, describing God creating the world. The root idea of this name is strength. Like Abraham generations earlier, David was "fully convinced that what He had promised He was also able to perform" (Romans 4:21).

God would likely honor His word and expand Israel's borders through military conflict. As a soldier, David understood this was the primary means by which national boundaries are extended. Although he and his generals would lead Israel into battle, David recognized Who was ultimately in control. He described God using another name, "LORD of hosts," which refers to God as the ultimate captain over all Israel's armies as well as the armies of heaven.

David expressed the driving motivation for his life when he prayed, "So let Your name be magnified forever" (2 Samuel 7:26). This was a constant theme in many of his psalms. For David, this goal was at the heart of everything he did.

GREAT LEADERS GIVE PRIORITY TO BRINGING GLORY TO GOD

COUNTING ON THE PROMISE OF GOD

David concluded his prayer with an affirmation of his belief that God would be faithful to keep His promises. "And now, O Lord GOD, You are God, and Your words are true, and You have promised this goodness to Your servant. Now therefore, let it please You to bless the house of Your servant, that it may continue before You forever; for You, O Lord GOD, have spoken it, and with Your blessing let the house of Your servant be blessed forever" (2 Samuel 7:28, 29).

In the weeks and months following this encounter with God, David took specific action based on his assurance of God's promise. Initially, he launched a series of battles against various enemies of Israel. His victories resulted in the expanded territory God had promised. But God had made another promise that was close to his heart. His son would someday build the temple that he longed to build. While God had not permitted him to build it, David would spend much of the rest of his life preparing materials to ensure that the temple would be worthy of the God who would be worshipped there.

GREAT LEADERS BELIEVE GOD AND ACT ON THE ASSURANCE HE WILL HONOR HIS WORD

David had accumulated great influence and wealth throughout his life, especially during his years as king. In one of his psalms, he confessed, "The earth is the LORD's, and all its fullness, the world and those who dwell therein" (Psalm 24:1). Therefore, it was surely not difficult for David to use his own wealth and influences to gather the resources his son would need to build the Temple.

First, David enlisted the services of "the aliens who were in the land of Israel" (1 Chronicles 22:2). These men were trained and assigned to work as stonemasons, quarrying the stones that would be the building blocks of the Temple. Then he began gathering metals, iron for the gates and nails that would be needed and bronze for the more decorative needs of the Temple. Large cedars from Tyre and Sidon were harvested so they could be dried and cut for lumber.

David knew his son Solomon was "young and inexperienced" and believed this temple should "be exceedingly magnificent, famous and glorious throughout all countries" (1 Chronicles 22:5). Therefore, he not only made preparations by gathering the necessary building materials, he shared his vision and passion for the project with Solomon. Then he gathered the leaders of Israel that would outlive him and called on them to support his son in this project. "Now set your heart and your soul to seek the LORD your God. Therefore arise and build the sanctuary of the LORD God, to bring the ark of the covenant of the LORD and the holy articles of God into the house that is to be built for the name of the LORD" (1 Chronicles 22:19).

GREAT LEADERS
TAKE TIME TO PLAN AND
PREPARE FOR GREAT UNDERTAKINGS

The kind of project David envisioned was immense. Building the physical structure would be challenging enough, but David was not interested in building a non-functioning cathedral to his God. Though it would not be built in his lifetime, David could still envision this temple as the functioning worship center of Israel. God's promise of expanded territorial boundaries and a reign of peace for Solomon implied that the nation itself would realize a significant population increase. It would be a human resource director's nightmare to enlist, train, and supervise the number of workers necessary to ensure that the nation's needs would be met. Thus, toward the end of his life, David began organizing his people to be certain that necessary tasks would be accomplished in an orderly manner for generations to come. Many of the structures he set in place survived the Babylonian Captivity and remained through the time of Christ.

David began with the Levites. By the end of his reign, he had twenty-four thousand Levites trained to work in the Temple, whom he organized, along with the priests descendent from Aaron, into divisions. They were given specific responsibilities to be fulfilled during their times of duty in the Temple. Then he organized the rest of the Levites to be responsible for other areas of ministry.

One significant aspect of ministry in the Temple was worship in song. Those who were skilled in vocal and instrumental music were organized into ministry teams under selected worship leaders. This aspect of worship was close David's heart, as he wrote over seventy psalms that were used in Temple worship. Many of those who led the worship teams were also among those who contributed to the recorded Psalms, including Asaph, Jeduthun and Heman.

No detail was overlooked in the preparation of this building that would house the worship of God. Some Levites were trained in and assigned to gate-keeping duties in both the Temple and city.

While some might view this position as insignificant, these men were responsible for crowd control and traffic flow, making certain that the worship of God would be conducted in an orderly manner, especially when large crowds arrived in Jerusalem for the feasts. Still others were assigned responsibilities in the treasuries, ensuring that the finances of the Temple were also managed well. Though much of David's interest focused on organizing the Temple staff, he also reorganized his military and political staff for greater efficiency. Although Solomon's reign was surely to be characterized by peace, it would have been irresponsible for Israel to disband its armed forces. Knowing he had greater insight into human character than his young son, David placed men whom he considered reliable in various positions of responsibility throughout the kingdom. This would give Solomon time to concentrate on ruling the kingdom in the early days of his reign, knowing he could depend on those whom his father had placed in positions of influence.

GREAT LEADERS ARE GREAT MANAGERS OF HUMAN RESOURCES

PASSING ON DREAMS TO THE NEXT GENERATION

With everything in place to ensure a smooth transition of power, David took time to challenge Solomon and others in prominent positions throughout the kingdom to pass on his dream to the next generation. He gathered the leaders of the kingdom together in a solemn assembly, in order to share with them his vision. He reminded them how it had been his desire to build the Temple, but God had said "No." He went on to explain how God had chosen Solomon to reign as successor and build His Temple.

As much as David wanted to talk about the Temple, he knew there was no use building the Temple if the nation lost its zeal for God. "Now therefore," he declared, "in the sight of all Israel, the assembly of the LORD, and in the hearing of our God, be careful to seek out all the commandments of the LORD your God, that you may possess this good land, and leave it as an inheritance for your children after you forever" (1 Chronicles 28:9).

David knew that the nation's zeal for God would likely never rise above that of their king. Turning to Solomon, he continued, "As for you, my son Solomon, know the God of your father, and serve Him with a loyal heart and with a willing mind; for the LORD searches all hearts and understands all the intent of the thoughts. If you seek Him, He will be found by you; but if you forsake Him, He will cast you off forever" (1 Chronicles 28:9).

Then David challenged his son concerning the building of the Temple. "Consider now, for the LORD has chosen you to build a house for the sanctuary; be strong and do it" (1 Chronicles 28:10). There was little more David needed to say about the matter as far as his son was concerned. David had prepared detailed plans for the construction of the building and had spent much of his latter years collecting everything needed to build the structure. Now it would be up to his son to implement the plans that had been made and use the resources that had been collected to build a temple worthy of Israel's God.

GREAT LEADERS PROMOTE GREAT DREAMS THAT WILL OUTLIVE THEM

David had already provided what would be necessary for the building of the Temple; he understood there was a risk that others might view it as his temple rather than the national center for worship. Also, there might be some in the nation tempted to use this accumulated wealth for other projects. Therefore, David addressed the assembly and recounted the wealth he was now placing in his son's hands, reminding them of the purpose of these materials. He challenged them to participate in the dream in a practical way. "Who then is willing to consecrate himself this day to the LORD?" (1 Chronicles 29:5).

The response was everything David had certainly hoped it would be. The national leadership quickly and publicly committed their involvement. Then they gave of their own financial resources in an offering taken to add to David's resources and be used for the building of the Temple. "They gave for the work of the house of God five thousand talents and ten thousand darics of gold, ten thousand talents of silver, eighteen thousand talents of bronze, and one hundred thousand talents of iron. And whoever had precious stones gave them to the treasury of the house of the LORD, into the hand of Jehiel the Gershonite" (1 Chronicles 29:7, 8). This free-will offering was a tangible expression of their commitment to God.

GREAT LEADERS INVITE OTHERS TO BELIEVE AND BE A PART OF THEIR DREAMS

David rejoiced when he saw the response of his people. He would not build the temple, but the people's commitment convinced him that it would be built soon. From deep within, he expressed his praise and worship to God. "Yours, O LORD, is the greatness, the power and the glory, the victory and the majesty; for all that is in heaven and in earth is Yours; Yours is the kingdom, O LORD, and You are exalted over all" (1 Chronicles 29:11).

There was little more David could do in preparation. He once again dedicated all that had been given to God. Now the building of the Temple would be the responsibility of others. One more time he prayed, "And give my son Solomon a loyal heart to keep Your commandments and Your testimonies and Your statutes, to do all these things and to build the temple for which I have made provision" (1 Chronicles 29:19).

GREAT LEADERS YIELD MATTERS TO GOD THAT ARE BEYOND THEIR CONTROL

CHAPTER NINE

WHEN YOU CAN FINALLY GET EVEN WITH THOSE WHO HINDERED YOU

2 Samuel 8:1-10:19; 1 Chronicles 18:1-19:19

Encouraged with the promised blessing of God upon his kingdom, David soon began working to expand Israel's territorial boundaries. The most obvious barrier to establishing a kingdom stretching from the Mediterranean Sea to the Euphrates River was Israel's historic enemy, the Philistines. They occupied the coastal plain territory, and from that region they had continually been a threat to Israel's security for generations. David knew he could not send his army far from home until he first dealt with the threat nearby.

GREAT LEADERS BELIEVE THE PROMISES OF GOD AND ACT ACCORDINGLY

David's initial popularity in Israel had been a result of his first battle with the Philistines in the Valley of Elah. There he defeated Goliath, a giant from Gath, one of the five principle cities of the region. In planning this new campaign against the Philistines, defeating Gath became a key objective. The battle plan was executed well and the Philistines were subdued. In the

159

end, David "took Gath and its towns from the hand of the Philistines" (1 Chronicles 18:1).

One account of David's victory over the Philistines describes just how effective Israel was in subduing their historic enemy. In this report, David is credited with taking "Metheg Ammah from the hand of the Philistines" (2 Samuel 8:1). The name "Metheg Ammah" references "the bridal of the mother city." The statement suggests David attacked and was victorious over the very heart of Philistia. When the battle was over, there was no more desire for war on their part.

While the victory over Philistia was important to the security of Israel, there was another threat on the eastern front that needed to be dealt with. The plains of Moab rose beyond the southeast shore of the Dead Sea and were clearly visible from southern Israel. Israel's conflict with Moab began as the nation completed its forty years in the wilderness and prepared to enter the Promised Land. Moab refused Israel passage through its territory, forcing the people to take an alternate route to the Jordan River.

Moab's threat to Israel's security went beyond any military strength the nation possessed. Its visibility was a subtle reminder to those living in the south of the nearby danger. Even if Moab never attacked, their close presence was a constant reminder that they could. David understood that Israel would never really feel safe as long as their most visible enemy remained unchallenged.

David launched his campaign against Moab and was once again victorious. In the course of the battle and its aftermath, a large part of Moab's population was eliminated. Those who survived the slaughter "became David's servants, and brought tribute" (1 Chronicles 18:2).

Years earlier, David had sought refuge in both Philistia and Moab. As a fugitive responsible for protecting his family and followers, David had hidden among the enemies of Israel at a time when he knew Israel was too weak to overcome their enemies. During that time, he no doubt gained valuable insights that he used in planning these battles. Now, as Israel's king, it was his responsibility to protect the nation from those who threatened its national security.

GREAT LEADERS DEAL WITH THE THREAT CLOSE TO HOME BEFORE TAKING ON MORE DISTANT CHALLENGES

FROM VICTORY TO VICTORY

Having dealt with the threat close to home, David could now take on more ambitious campaigns that promised to stretch Israel's territorial boundaries toward those described in his recent covenant with God. In his next battle he faced Hadadezer, king of Zorba. Zorba's territory stretched east as far as the Euphrates River. A victory against this king would extend Israel's borders farther than they had ever been before.

Although this new battle differed significantly from those against Philistia and Moab, the previous victories encouraged David's men to believe victory was possible. Encouraged by their previous success, they marched forward and once again proved successful in battle. The record of the prisoners of war taken in battle indicates the strength of the enemy. "David took from him one thousand chariots, seven thousand horsemen, and twenty thousand foot soldiers" (1 Chronicles 18:4).

Prior to David's invasion, Zorba had formed an alliance with Syria. While the two nations had their differences, they both viewed David as a common threat and had agreed to defend each other from hostile action from Israel. But the aid of Syria did nothing to help Zorba and earned for David yet another military victory. "When the Syrians of Damascus came to help Hadadezer king of Zorba, David killed twenty-two thousand of the Syrians" (1 Chronicles 18:5).

While these battles were taking place in the northeast, David's army was also dealing with another threat in the south. Under the leadership of Abishai the son of Zeruiah, they were victorious in battle over Edom in the Valley of Salt, near the Dead Sea. Eighteen thousand Edomites fell in that battle (1 Chronicles 18:12).

Nothing motivates people to succeed like success. Each victory encouraged Israel's army to believe that the next battle could also be won. In contrast, the significant defeats experienced by Israel's enemies discouraged them from considering a revolt against their new rulers. From victory to victory, David strengthened and expanded the borders of his kingdom.

GREAT LEADERS BUILD ON PAST VICTORIES TO ENCOURAGE OTHERS IN THE PURSUIT OF NEW CHALLENGES

While this series of military victories expanded Israel's borders, it also created new potential problems. There were now many people living within the nation who had no natural loyalty to the nation. Further, these people knew it was possible for them to live independently of the nation, as they already had their own social infrastructure in place. Even if these populations seemed content to dwell in Israel right now, there was no guarantee they would remain that way.

Understanding this danger, David adopted a two-fold strategy to make certain that no insurrections would occur. First, he took steps to disarm those he conquered. In his victory over Hadadezer, David seized shields of gold and large quantities of bronze and silver. Rather than leave these materials among those who could use it in battle against David, they were stored in Jerusalem for future use in the building of the temple.

But disarming his enemies involved more than simply removing weapons and materials that could be used to make new weapons. It also meant ensuring that a rebel army would not have the mobility it once had. Under Jewish law, the kings of Israel were forbidden to "multiply horses for himself" (Deuteronomy 17:16). The number of horses had placed Israel at a disadvantage when facing a nation like Zorba, which had a large cavalry. Part of disarming that nation involved hamstringing most of their horses. This preserved the life of the horse yet made it virtually useless for military purposes.

GREAT LEADERS ACT TO ENSURE POTENTIAL ENEMIES ARE NOT STRONG ENOUGH TO DO HARM

Commenting on this period in the life of David, F. B. Meyer noted, "It is thus in every era of the history of God's people that Satan has stirred up their foes. Right behind the coalitions of men lies the malignity of the fallen spirit who ever seeks to bruise the heel of the woman's seed."[1] David understood that the victories he achieved on the battlefields were a spiritual gift from God. As the Lord's anointed king, his real enemy was the enemy of God. Other nations were merely mannequins whose strings were being pulled by the devil. His victories over Israel's enemies were in reality spiritual victories.

In recognition of this truth, David allocated the plunder and tribute he received from his former enemies to the treasury of the temple. Though he had been denied the privilege of building the temple, he was determined to do all he could to ensure his son would have all the resources necessary to build a house worthy of the God to be worshipped there. In devoting this wealth to that purpose, he was recognizing that it was the Lord who "preserved David wherever he went" (1 Chronicles 18:6, 13).

GREAT LEADERS ARE QUICK TO ACKNOWLEDGE GOD'S ROLE IN THEIR GREAT VICTORIES

INTERNATIONAL RECOGNITION

David's decisive military action probably minimized the death and destruction of otherwise inevitable future wars. As other nations recognized David's will to fight and the ability of Israel to be victorious in battle, they chose to form new alliances with Israel rather than confront them on the battlefield. Tou, king of Hamath, was one who elected this response toward Israel. "He sent Hadoram his son to King David, to greet him and bless him, because he had fought against Hadadezer and defeated him" (1 Chronicles 18:10).

The king of Hamath especially wanted to form an alliance with David because Hadadezer had formerly defeated them. That defeat most likely resulted in the country being looted, leading citizens being enslaved, and an annual tribute being paid to the victorious king. Now that Hadadezer had been defeated by David, Hamath was experiencing both political and economic liberty. When King Tou's son arrived in Jerusalem for a state visit, he bore gifts of gold, silver, and bronze. These gifts were also added to the nation's treasury for future use in the building of the temple.

Hamath was only the first of many former subjects of Hadadezer to form an alliance with David. After Israel was victorious in a later battle against Syrian mercenaries and the Ammonites, others followed his example. "And when all the kings who were servants to Hadadezer saw that they were defeated by Israel, they made peace with Israel and served them" (2 Samuel 10:19).

Throughout his life, David fought the battles his son Solomon would never have to face. His success on the battlefield earned him and his nation a reputation that would outlive the king. While David experienced some of the benefits of that reputation, his son was the real benefactor. By the time Solomon assumed the throne, tribute was coming from nations scattered throughout the region. An army was maintained in Israel under Solomon's reign, but it was not tested in battle. Because their success had been proven under David's leadership, it was simply assumed they could defeat anyone who challenged them.

GREAT LEADERS ESTABLISH A REPUTATION OTHERS COME TO RESPECT

ESTABLISHING INTERNAL STABILITY

Establishing a stable government was necessary in order to maintain the victories achieved on the battlefield as well as provide for the security and efficient administration of the nation. As David rose to his zenith of power, he took actions on both fronts. He established a homeland security strategy to protect the nation from internal problems, and entrusted the administration of his national affairs to individuals who had proven committed to their king.

David's new homeland security strategy involved the establishment of military outposts throughout his newly acquired territory. These outposts housed troops who would be the first line of defense in the event of an insurrection. These troops could deal with the immediate threat until reinforcements arrived to put down the rebellion completely. Army garrisons were assigned in both Damascus (1 Chronicles 18:6) and Edom (1 Chronicles 18:13).

David's choice of Damascus and Edom demonstrated insight into the areas most likely to act as centers of rebellion in the kingdom. It would be Damascus that, centuries later, would take the northern kingdom of Israel into captivity. Throughout history, Edom demonstrated hostility toward Israel in at least seventeen recorded conflicts prior to the fall of Jerusalem. If an insurrection were to develop during David's reign, these were the two most likely places that rebellion would begin.

GREAT LEADERS REMAIN AWARE OF POTENTIAL PROBLEMS

"So David reigned over all Israel; and David administered

judgment and justice to all his people" (2 Samuel 8:15). David ruled efficiently by entrusting various responsibilities to others and granting them the authority they needed to act on his behalf. He gathered around him those whom he trusted most, including close family members and men who had proven their loyalty in battle. His cousin Joab had primary responsibility over the army. Others assumed major roles within the priesthood and recording the national history. His own sons were incorporated into this governing cabinet. One of his warriors, Beniah, was given authority over the Cherethites and Pelethites, and eventually was responsible for palace security.

The choosing of Beniah for such an important responsibility helps to illustrate the kind of man David looked for in his leaders. Beniah was the son of a successful soldier, but he was chosen for his own accomplishments. He "had killed two lion-like heroes of Moab. He also had gone down and killed a lion in the midst of a pit on a snowy day. And he killed an Egyptian, a spectacular man. The Egyptian had a spear in his hand; so he went down to him with a staff, wrestled the spear out of the Egyptian's hand, and killed him with his own spear" (2 Samuel 23:20, 21). In each instance, Beniah faced an apparently impossible task and found a way to prevail. He was the kind of man who did not ask, "Can that be done?" when given an assignment, rather asking, "How can that be done?" With men like Beniah in leadership, David knew the kingdom was in good hands.

GREAT LEADERS DELEGATE RESPONSIBILITY AND AUTHORITY TO CAPABLE LEADERS

EXTENDING GRACE TOWARD MEPHIBOSHETH

David's recent victories and reorganization of his cabinet placed him in the strongest position of his career. While there would be other battles fought and challenges faced, there were no real threats to Israel's security and he had absolute authority within the kingdom itself. In many cultures, these conditions tend to result in a purging of the nation. When a ruler is strong enough to act independently of internal public opinion and external military threats, he often takes the opportunity to eliminate any real and perceived opposition to his agenda. This is often a very bloody time in a nation's history.

Had he decided to do so, David certainly could now exact vengeance upon many people. There were siblings from his family whom he could now get even with. Years earlier, those who then had power in the nation had forced him into exile as a fugitive. When he was finally crowned king in Judah, the northern tribes of Israel had resisted his right to the throne for years. No doubt in the years since there had been individuals whose actions failed to measure up to what David had hoped for. If he should choose to purge the nation of his enemies, real and perceived, there would be many eliminated in the process.

But now, when David could finally get revenge, he chose not to use his power for that purpose. Rather, the bitterness that often consumes those who struggle to achieve such a level of success had been forced out by a heart full of appreciation toward those who had helped him succeed. This attitude of gratitude proved to act as the source of what many Bible teachers believe was David's greatest hour.

Gratitude may be described as the acid test of character. As parents strive to shape their child's character, one goal is to train that child to express appreciation and gratitude for favors received. Parents want their children to show gratitude because it is the right thing to do.

Learning to express gratitude to others can also assist in the worship of God. Giving thanksgiving to God allows for Him to be praised. David urged his people, "Enter into His gates with thanksgiving, and into His courts with praise. Be thankful to Him and bless His name" (Psalm 100:4). This was the beginning of the worship experience of Israel as they gathered in Jerusalem.

No one person is an island. Those who experience success in

life do so because of the assistance of others. They may also experience opposition from others along their journey, but they have a choice of which group they decide to remember. David could have chosen to remember that Saul had tried to kill him, but instead he chose to remember how Jonathan had been there to help. Now that he had the power to act, David honored his covenant with Jonathan and expressed gratitude to the former royal family rather than use his power to retaliate against them for Saul's treatment of him.

GREAT LEADERS KNOW NOT TO USE POWER TO THEIR OWN ADVANTAGE

As David considered how to express his gratitude for all Jonathan had done, he had to look beyond his usual advisors for help. Those most closely associated with Saul had gone into hiding, due to the usual custom of kings to destroy anyone associated with a former government. David's advisors were not aware if any members of Saul's family were still alive, but eventually they discovered one of Saul's advisors who might have the answers they sought. They found Ziba and brought him to Jerusalem to meet David.

Ziba was likely very uncomfortable when first approached by David's men. When he realized they knew who he was, he immediately described himself as being available to serve David. Perhaps he hoped he could somehow demonstrate his loyalty to David and avoid his suspected fate. As he stood before the king, he must have been stunned by David asking, "Is there not still someone of the house of Saul, to whom I may show the kindness of God?" (1 Samuel 9:3).

"There is still a son of Jonathan who is lame in his feet," Ziba answered (1 Samuel 9:3). As the discussion continued, Ziba told David about Mephibosheth, who lived in an undesirable part of the nation described as Lo Debar, the place of no pasture. This child of hope who had been born into the royal family, in direct line to assume the throne from his father, had been crippled as a young child. His nurse had dropped him as she hastily pursued safety when news of Saul's death reached Gibeah (2 Samuel 4:4). About that time, his name had been changed to Mephibosheth. The key element in his new name reflected the change in his status from that of a "master" to one covered in "shame."

When David learned about Mephibosheth and his situation, he faced a difficult decision. Choosing to express gratitude is never easy. The human tendency toward self-centeredness needs to be overcome by a conscious effort to put others first. Also, an expression of gratitude often comes at a cost. To care for Mephibosheth would cost David. In addition, if conditions changed and an uprising against David occurred, Mephibosheth was a potential rival. Even if he did not lead an insurrection, others could use him to gain support and legitimacy for their attempted coup.

The greatest barrier to David proceeding with his intention to express gratitude to Jonathan's family was Mephibosheth's physical condition. When David took Jerusalem from the Jebusites, they had claimed "the blind and the lame" would successfully defend the city (2 Samuel 5:6). Although that did not happen, the blind and the lame were subsequently described as those "who are hated by David's soul," and a popular proverb stated, "The blind and the lame shall not come into the house" (2 Samuel 5:8). To extend grace to Mephibosheth, David would have to overcome a significant social stigma attached to the lame.

The issue needed to be considered, yet David's calling as Israel's king required that he support the disenfranchised of society. This was one of the ways Israel would remain different from the nations around her. As part of his training to rule as Israel's king, David's son Solomon was told, "Open your mouth for the speechless, in the cause of all who are appointed to die. Open your mouth, judge righteously, and plead the cause of the poor and needy" (Proverbs 31:8, 9).

GREAT LEADERS SUPPORT THE DISENFRANCHISED IN SOCIETY

Mephibosheth came from a royal family that did not share David's values in regards to caring for the poor and needy. When he was summoned to the palace, he no doubt concluded his days were numbered. When he arrived in David's presence, "he fell on his face and prostrated himself" (2 Samuel 9:6). When he was called by name, he identified himself only as David's servant. As David began speaking further, only then did Mephibosheth begin realizing this day would probably not conclude as he anticipated. David had a different agenda in mind.

David began the meeting with his friend's son with an offer of forgiveness. He would not hold the lame man responsible for his grandfather's acts. "Do not fear," David encouraged, explaining, "I will surely show you kindness for Jonathan your father's sake, and will restore to you all the land of Saul your grandfather" (2 Samuel 9:7).

Beyond forgiveness, David extended the hand of fellowship. "You shall eat bread at my table continually," he added (2 Samuel 9:7). David understood that fractured relationships are not really reconciled until both parties can sit together and enjoy a meal. To demonstrate that he held no ill will toward Saul's family, David invited Mephibosheth to be his constant dinner guest.

David's act of kindness changed Mephibosheth's fortunes dramatically. He would no longer live in poverty and obscurity. David made his previous private promise to restore the land of Saul public when he appointed Ziba as steward responsible for the management of those properties on Mephibosheth's behalf. The lame man from the land of no pastures would not only own vast pastures, he would have servants to manage his growing flocks and herds on those pastures.

Mephibosheth had lost his father, grandfather and uncles in battle when he was just a young child. Though others had cared for him and helped him throughout life, he never enjoyed the privileges of being part of the royal family, a destiny that was his at birth. That too would change as a result of David's kindness. "As for Mephibosheth," David explained, "he shall eat at my table like one of the king's sons" (2 Samuel 9:11).

Although he would not realize it for years to come, Mephibosheth also received David's pledge of fidelity that day. David and Jonathan had established a covenant years earlier that prompted this action. Just as David had been faithful to his promise to Jonathan, so he would remain faithful to his promise to Mephibosheth. Even years later, after Mephibosheth is slandered and identified as one who sides in a rebellion against the king, David remains faithful and treats him kindly (2 Samuel 19:28-30).

JUST LIKE JESUS

David's treatment of Mephibosheth was more than an expression of gratitude for Jonathan's assistance; in many ways David modeled the very character of Jesus, who is also called, "the Son of David" (Matthew 1:1). Though not specifically identified as such in the New Testament, many Bible teachers see this account as an example of God's treatment of sinners. Several parallels become apparent with a closer look at the biblical text.

The chapter begins with "now David said" (2 Samuel 9:1). David took the initiative in looking for Mephiboseth. In the New Testament, Jesus told the woman at the well, "the Father is seeking such to worship Him" (John 4:23).

David's goal was to find someone "left of the house of Saul" (2 Samuel 9:1). Saul was David's enemy just as sinners stand in enmity against God. "But God demonstrated His own love toward us, in that while we were still sinners, Christ died for us" (Romans 5:8). Paul added, "For if when we were enemies we were reconciled to God through the death of His Son, much more, having been reconciled, we shall be saved by His life" (Romans 5:10).

David expressed his motivation for finding someone from Saul's family with the words, "that I may show him kindness" (2 Samuel

9:1). Once again, this is God's motive in seeking sinners and demonstrating His grace to them. "Even when we were dead in trespasses, [God] made us alive together with Christ . . . that in the ages to come He might show the exceeding riches of His grace in His kindness toward us in Christ Jesus" (Ephesians 2:5, 7).

Mephibosheth was lame, therefore he could not help himself. In the New Testament, those outside of Christ are described as "dead in trespasses and sins" (Ephesians 2:1). There is nothing we can do to help ourselves.

Prior to being called into the palace, Mephibosheth was living in a place called Lo-debar, the place of "no pasture." Those outside of Christ likewise live in a place without blessing, spiritual food, provision or protection. While many might turn to the Twenty-Third Psalm for comfort, they have no place in the pasture until the Lord is indeed their Shepherd.

When he learned about Mephibosheth, "then King David sent and brought him out" (2 Samuel 9:5). The initiative in this situation was that of David, just as God initiated Christ coming into the world "to save that which was lost" (Matthew 18:11).

The name Mephibosheth means "shameful things." The Scriptures describe people as conceived in sin. The closer one looks at the darkness and sin of the human heart, the more this designation can be applied to sinners without Christ.

David brought Mephibosheth into the palace of the king. All who come to faith in Christ will someday realize Mephibosheth's experience. Jesus said, "In My Father's house are many mansions; if it were not so, I would have told you. I go to prepare a place for you" (John 14:2).

David's first words to Mephibosheth as he announced his plans were, "Do not fear" (2 Samuel 9:7). Jesus began His Upper Room Discourse, His final message before the cross, with the words, "Let not your heart be troubled" (John 14:1).

David promised to "restore to you all the land of Saul your grandfather" (2 Samuel 9:7). All that had been lost through Saul's sin and fall would be recovered. In comparing the effects of Adam's sin and Christ's obedience, Paul demonstrated that everything lost to the human race in the fall could be recovered in Christ because of the cross (Romans 5:12-21).

Finally, David promised Mephibosheth, "you shall eat bread at my table continually" (2 Samuel 9:7). The New Testament teaches, "For all the promises of God in Him are Yes, and in Him Amen, to the glory of God through us" (2 Corinthians 1:20). One of those promises states, "Surely goodness and mercy shall follow me all the days of my life; and I will dwell in the house of the LORD forever" (Psalm 23:6).

GREAT LEADERS MODEL THE CHARACTER OF THE GREATEST LEADER

AN ACT OF GRACE REJECTED

Though reluctant to accept the honor, Mephibosheth consented to David's gracious offer. "So Mephibosheth dwelt in Jerusalem, for he ate continually at the king's table" (2 Samuel 9:13). He was still lame, but as the recipient of the king's grace his status in life had changed dramatically. But there were others not so eager to accept David's gracious gestures.

During this period of David's reign, Nahash, king of Ammon, died and his son Hanun assumed the throne. Nahash had been an ally of David and close personal friend. Much as one might send condolences to family members of a departed friend, David decided to "show kindness to Hanun the son of Nahas, as his father showed kindness to" him (2 Samuel 10:2). He sent a delegation to the new king to attempt to comfort him in the death of his father.

Unfortunately, those gathered to advise Hanun in the affairs of state were suspicious of David and were unwilling to believe he would be so gracious during the transition in their nation. "Do you think that David really honors your father because he has sent comforters to you?" they questioned. "Has David not rather sent his servants to you to search the city, to spy it out, and to overthrow it?" (2 Samuel 10:3).

The young king was easily persuaded and made a terrible decision. When David's men arrived, they were publicly humiliated and sent back to Israel. Knowing that facial hair was a sign of masculinity in Semitic cultures, the king ordered that half their face be shaved. Beyond this, before sending them off, he cut the garments they were wearing so that their buttocks were exposed as they walked.

When David heard about this insult to his delegation, he left Jerusalem and met with the men privately in Jericho. Perhaps he found it hard to believe any ruler could act so irresponsibly and wanted to see for himself. When he realized the report was true, he determined that his men should not be embarrassed any further. He told them to remain in Jericho until their beards grew back. As David left the meeting, it was difficult to hide his anger. But before David could think of an appropriate response to this action, the Ammonites left him no option but to engage in battle.

GREAT LEADERS KNOW THE PAIN OF HAVING THEIR MOTIVES MISJUDGED BY OTHERS

"When the people of Ammon saw that they had made themselves repulsive to David, the people of Ammon sent and hired the Syrians of Beth Rehob and the Syrians of Zoba, twenty thousand foot soldiers and from the king of Maacah one thousand men, and from Is-Tob twelve thousand men" (2 Samuel 10:6). This overwhelming force was arranged on the battlefield surrounding the army of Israel. Their intentions were obvious and Israel was desperate.

Despite Israel's previous victories, there appeared no guarantee of success in this battle. Joab surveyed the situation quickly and made a strategic decision. "When Joab saw that the battle line was against him before and behind, he chose some of Israel's best and put them in battle array against the Syrians. And the rest of the people he put under the command of Abishai his brother, that he might set them in battle array against the people of Ammon" (2 Samuel 10:9, 10). Each force fought a separate battle, forcing the enemy to fight on two fronts. He decided that when one division won its battle it would then join the other to assist in the battle. However, this part of the battle plan never occurred.

Joab and Israel's best soldiers attacked the Syrians with everything they had. Although the Syrians had come to the aid of an ally, this was not really their battle. As a result, they were less committed to the cause than the Ammonites and quickly withdrew from the battle. At the same time, Abishai and his larger army of less experienced soldiers attacked the Ammonites. When the Ammonites saw their ally retreating from the battlefield, they too fled. Once again Israel experienced victory in battle with her enemies.

David was now firmly established in the kingdom. While there were still cities to be conquered, the nation's army held a firm reputation of superiority over its foes. Many nations had formed alliances with Israel to avoid being conquered by its army. The people of Israel lived securely within its borders and experienced the blessing of God upon the nation. It seemed like everything was going right, but very soon everything would be wrong. Few would have guessed the source of the impending disaster.

CHAPTER TEN

WHEN YOU BEGIN TO LET SUCCESS GO TO YOUR HEAD

2 Samuel 11:1-13:39; 1 Chronicles 20:1-8; Psalms 32; 38; 51

When everything seems to be going right or at least moving in the right direction, unexpected problems tend to have a greater impact than if their threat had been recognized earlier. Perhaps that is why Paul warned the Corinthians, "Therefore let him who thinks he stands take heed lest he fall" (1 Corinthians 10:12). It is unfortunate this warning came too late to be heeded by David.

Throughout much of David's life, the threat of danger had been a constant. From the day the young shepherd first defended his flock from a predator, he knew life would not be easy. As a soldier, the threat was even more extreme. Even as a king, David continued leading his men into battle and had to remain alert to possible attempts to usurp the throne. For years, he had struggled and had succeeded because he recognized and dealt with problems as they emerged.

But things were different now. The kingdom was well established, larger and stronger than it had ever been before. Enemies who had threatened Israel's existence in the past had been destroyed or disarmed and were no longer a real threat. There were still battles to be fought, but on a much smaller scale than those which had already resulted in victory. Internally, the nation was at peace and supported the leadership of their king. David had built his palace and, though not permitted to build a temple for the worship of God, he was comforted by the fact that this personal goal would be realized a generation later. David could now enjoy the fruit of his labor in relative comfort and ease.

So it was that in the best of times, David fell. He did not fall in one of the areas with which he had struggled for years. Like others throughout history, David failed at the point of his strength. The king, consumed with an intense passion for God, was sidetracked by an illegitimate passion for another man's wife. In the final analysis, David had no one to blame for his sin but himself. Though it took some time, eventually David himself recognized this to be true.

GREAT LEADERS RECOGNIZE THAT THEY ARE NOT PERFECT

A ROYAL AFFAIR

As winter ended and the weather warmed with the coming of spring, the number of conflicts between cities and kingdoms tended to increase. There were several reasons for this phenomenon in that age. First, winter weather and cold temperatures were conditions that made it difficult for soldiers to fight effectively. The extra clothing that needed to be worn to stay warm hindered their mobility in the battle, and winter storms could easily disrupt supply lines. Second, because battles were not fought in winter, unresolved disputes from the previous season often led to a hardening of positions in conflicts that might otherwise have been resolved. This resulted in spring conflicts over comparatively minor issues. Beyond this, there was the spring harvest. Many conflicts in that age concerned food. Since reserves were consumed in winter, armies often invaded to loot the spring harvest.

When the spring season began, the battles that remained for

Israel were only minor. Significant victories had been won against the Ammonites, but Rabbah remained unconquered. Every indication showed that the royal city would not surrender and would have to be defeated. The most effective way to accomplish this goal involved laying siege to the capital. David recognized the battle needed to be fought, but chose not to lead it directly. Instead, he sent his army under the command of Joab. David might have avoided the sinful situation that would occur, had he led his troops into battle, which was his responsibility as king.

David may not have been getting the rest he needed to be alert and make good decisions. There were times when he went to bed and did not fall asleep immediately, or woke up after only a brief rest. On one of those occasions, "David arose from his bed and walked on the roof of the king's house" (2 Samuel 11:2). Some Bible teachers think David may have gone to the roof to enjoy the cool spring breezes. Others think he went to look over his city. From his roof, he could see everything that was happening in the city and beyond.

As he looked out from his roof, one thing in particular caught his eye. "He saw a woman bathing, and the woman was very beautiful to behold" (2 Samuel 11:2). As his eyes glanced across the city, he may not have been able to avoid seeing this woman. But he did have a choice as to whether to continue looking. He chose not only to look, but also to make further inquiries into who this woman was. One of his servants recognized her and said, "Is this not Bathsheba, the daughter of Eliam, the wife of Uriah the Hittite?" (2 Samuel 11:3).

Uriah was a loyal soldier in David's army involved in the siege of Rabbah. It was unthinkable that his king would reward such loyal service with betrayal. Even if Uriah had not been a loyal soldier, the seventh commandment of the nation's governing law forbid extra-marital affairs (Exodus 20:14). But David was no longer thinking clearly or willing to submit to the restraints of the law. "Then David sent messengers, and took her; and she came to him, and he lay with her, for she was cleansed from her impurity" (2 Samuel 11:4).

David's actions were common behavior among kings in the Middle East, but God had designated Israel as a distinct people. The lifestyle standards for Jewish kings were much higher. The law had specifically forbidden such usual behavior of rulers (Deuteronomy 17:17). In any other capital, Bathsheba might have been given a place in the palace harem, but not in Jerusalem. When their night of passion ended, she returned home so others in the city would not learn of the incident.

GREAT LEADERS MAKE BAD DECISIONS WHEN DISTRACTED FROM THEIR PRIMARY TASK

THE COVER-UP

Perhaps only weeks later, David discovered that he had a major problem to deal with. Bathsheba realized she was pregnant. Since her husband had been on the battlefield for some time, there was no question in her mind who the father was. She discretely sent a note to David with a brief message, "I am with child" (2 Samuel 11:5).

Nothing more needed to be said. David knew exactly what the note meant. Within months, Bathsheba would be exposed as an adulteress. Under Jewish law, this would give Uriah the right to have her stoned. David was reasonably sure that she would identify him as her partner in passion in an attempt to preserve her life. He also knew that this would create a very difficult situation for him. As he considered the situation, he quickly developed a plan for resolution.

David received regular reports on the progress of the battle of Rabbah. He sent a message to Joab, ordering him to send Uriah the Hittite as the messenger bearing the next report. He had seen others who handled this assignment look forward to spending a night or two in their own bed with their wife. After months on the battlefield, he expected Uriah to also be eager to spend time with his beautiful wife. Then, when he learned several months later that Bathsheba had given birth, he would naturally assume he had fathered the child.

When Uriah arrived, David met with him to review the progress of the battle. When their meeting concluded, David thanked Uriah for the report and encouraged him to take advantage of being in Jerusalem and enjoy an evening in his own home. To ensure it would be an evening of celebration, David also sent food to his home for Uriah and Bathsheba to enjoy together. But David had underestimated Uriah's loyalty to him.

"But Uriah slept at the door of the king's house with all the servants of his lord, and did not go down to his house" (2 Samuel 11:9). When David heard this, he could not understand why a man would not take an opportunity to enjoy the comforts of home with his wife. When he met with Uriah later that day, he asked him directly. Uriah responded, "The ark and Israel and Judah are dwelling in tents, and my lord Joab and the servants of my lord are encamped in open fields. Shall I then go to my house to eat and drink, and to lie with my wife? As you live, and as your soul lives, I will not do this thing" (2 Samuel 11:11).

David had not counted on this kind of commitment from Uriah. Unfortunately, Uriah's loyalty was about to create greater problems for David. Still, there was hope the problem could be resolved. David delayed sending Uriah back to the front for a day and entertained him with food and wine. As the wine continued to flow, Uriah became increasingly more intoxicated. David likely hoped Uriah would wake from his drunken stupor the next morning next to Bathsheba, but the soldier once again slept in quarters. Unwilling to deal directly with his own actions, David had only one other way of settling this problem.

Just before Uriah was sent back to the front, he met with David and was given sealed orders to be delivered to Joab. He had no idea he was carrying orders that would cost him his life. David's orders to Joab read, "Set Uriah in the forefront of the hottest battle, and retreat from him, that he may be struck down and die" (2 Samuel 11:15). By eliminating Uriah, Bathsheba would never face an adultery charge and his risk of exposure would also be eliminated.

When Joab received the orders, he acted on them. An attack was scheduled on the city at the point Joab knew was their strongest defensive position. Uriah was among those assigned to that attack. As expected, Uriah was killed in battle along with several others in the army. When the mission had been accomplished, Joab sent a messenger back to Jerusalem with the report.

The continuation of David's sinful act played out in Jerusalem when the messenger arrived. David sent back a message encouraging Joab. "Do not let this thing displease you, for the sword devours one as well as another. Strengthen your attack against the city, and overthrow it" (2 Samuel 11:25). Those who did not know the rest of the story might have admired their king for being so consoling in the face of defeat.

News of Uriah's death was also delivered to Bathsheba. "When the wife of Uriah heard that Uriah her husband was dead, she mourned for her husband" (2 Samuel 11:26). After a reasonable period of mourning had passed, David invited Bathsheba back to the palace and she became one of his wives. When her term ended, she gave birth to a son. Everything seemed to have worked out in the end. It had taken a battle defeat and the deaths of several loyal soldiers, but David's adulterous affair had been successfully concealed.

There was only one problem: "The thing that David had done displeased the LORD" (2 Samuel 11:27).

GREAT LEADERS MAKE SITUATIONS WORSE WHEN THEY TRY TO CONCEAL THEIR FAILURES

THE PAIN OF SUCCESS

Although David had successfully hidden his sin from public exposure, he could not hide it from God. Neither could he break free of the fear that his sin might eventually be exposed. Even if no one else knew what he had done, he knew, and the secret began to grow into an evil infection he found increasingly more difficult to deal with. During the time he thought he should be feeling relief for accomplishing his goal, he was feeling something very different. The anguish of his soul is reflected in a few psalms many Bible teachers believe David wrote around this time.

"O LORD, do not rebuke me in Your wrath, nor chasten me in Your hot displeasure! For Your arrows pierce me deeply, and Your hand presses me down" (Psalm 38:1, 2). There was no doubt in David's mind that the scheme he thought had worked so well had failed to hide his sin from God. He knew enough about the character of God to know that hidden sin would not go unpunished and sensed the judicial hand of God already at work in his life.

Even though David knew that sin had to be dealt with, he delayed addressing the problem. This delay led to more serious consequences. "When I kept silent, my bones grew old through my groaning all the day long. For day and night Your hand was heavy upon me; my vitality was turned into the drought of summer" (Psalm 32:3, 4). He felt his energy being sapped out of his body, and experienced other physical problems normally associated with aging and the improper functioning of his immune system. "There is no soundness in my flesh because of Your anger, nor any health in my bones because of my sin. . . . My wounds are foul and festering because of my foolishness" (Psalm 38:3, 5).

David's description of the physical symptoms he experienced at that time suggest he may have contracted a sexually transmitted disease, a condition the Scriptures often warn about as a likely consequence of adultery. "I am troubled, I am bowed down greatly; I go mourning all the day long. For my loins are full of inflammation, and there is no soundness in my flesh. I am feeble and severely broken; I groan because of the turmoil of my heart. . . . My heart pants, my strength fails me; as for the light of my eyes, it also has gone from me" (Psalm 38:6-8, 10).

While many in ill health have the comfort of close friends and family members to help them through, those closest to David apparently feared his condition might be contagious and did their best to avoid any physical contact. "My loved ones and my friends stand aloof from my plague, and my relatives stand afar off" (Psalm 38:11). David began fearing that his enemies might take advantage of his weakness and attack.

There can be little doubt that David perceived his condition to be a judgment of God for his sin with Bathsheba; still he resisted addressing the situation. "But I, like a deaf man, do not hear; and I am like a mute who does not open his mouth. Thus I am like a man who does not hear, and in whose mouth is no response" (Psalm 38:13, 14). While others wondered why he was ill, David knew he had sinned and continued in his rebellious state even as he suffered emotionally and physically.

Some people change only when they hurt enough to want to change. Though it took some time, David eventually hit the bottom and began considering a different response to his sin. "For I am ready to fall, and my sorrow is continually before me. For I will declare my iniquity; I will be in anguish over my sin" (Psalm 38:17, 18).

GREAT LEADERS LIVE WITH THE KNOWLEDGE OF THEIR FAILURE EVEN WHEN OTHERS ARE UNAWARE

NATHAN'S PARABLE

Once David's hard heart had been softened, God gave Nathan the prophet a challenging assignment. "Surely the Lord GOD does nothing, unless He reveals His secret to His servants the prophets" (Amos 3:7). As a prophet of God, Nathan had often heard the voice of God. He was committed to faithfully reporting God's message to His people, good or bad, but this message was certainly not within the norm. He was given the assignment

of confronting the king and exposing the sin David had so carefully hidden from public view.

The fact that David had hidden his plot may have been reason
enough for Nathan to be reluctant to speak to the king. He knew
that David tended to administer quick and decisive judgment.
When the Amalekite claimed he had killed Saul, David had him
executed instantly because he had destroyed the Lord's anointed.
Later, when those responsible for the murder of Ish-bosheth
appeared before the king, he quickly had those assassins executed.
As Nathan considered his new assignment, he understood he might
not survive if David resisted his rebuke.

Nathan also knew that the continued prosperity of the nation
was a result of David's policies and actions. Exposing David's sin
might lead to unfavorable political and economic consequences,
sure to produce devastating effects on the national lifestyle. Was
Nathan prepared to be responsible for this possibility? And if it
happened this way, how would the people respond to the prophet
who had exposed the king and caused their suffering?

But these were not the most critical issues Nathan needed to
consider as he prepared for a visit to the palace. The reputation of
God was at stake. How could God bless a nation that hid an adul-
terer and murderer in the throne room? The very nature of the
prophetic office was that which defended the honor of God and
applied God's law to every situation without regard to other less
important considerations. Nathan's call as a prophet dictated his
response to God's revelation.

Nathan's duty was not only to report to David what God had
said, but also to do it in a way that David would hear and understand. While prophets sometimes spoke directly to a specific situation, often they had to share their message through symbolism for
the greatest impact. In this situation, Nathan decided to use a fabricated report about a poor man's sheep to get God's message across
to David. He likely hoped that David's shepherd background
would help him to identify with the poor man who lost his only
sheep and ultimately recognize how offensive his sin had been to

God.

Nathan stood before the king and began his story. "There were two men in one city, one rich and the other poor. The rich man had exceedingly many flocks and herds. But the poor man had nothing except one little ewe lamb which he bought and nourished; and it grew up together with him and with his children. It ate of his own food and drank from his own cup and lay in his bosom; and it was like a daughter to him. And a traveler came to the rich man, who refused to take from his own flock and from his own herd to prepare one for the wayfaring man who had come to him; but he took the poor man's lamb and prepared it for the man who had come to him" (2 Samuel 12:1-4).

David was incensed as he heard the report. In a state of rage, he turned to Nathan and quickly pronounced his sentence. "As the LORD lives, the man who has done this shall surely die! And he shall restore fourfold for the lamb, because he did this thing and because he had no pity" (2 Samuel 12:5, 6).

David's response convinced Nathan he had caught the king's attention. The moment of truth had come. Looking his king in the eyes, he announced, "You are the man!" (2 Samuel 12:7)

Nathan reminded his king of God's blessing upon him throughout his life and God's willingness to do even more if necessary. But God would not overlook this murderous and adulterous act. "You have killed Uriah the Hittite with the sword; you have taken his wife to be your wife, and have killed him with the sword of the people of Ammon" (2 Samuel 12:9).

Such sin would result in severe consequences. "Now therefore, the sword shall never depart from your house, because you have despised Me, and have taken the wife of Uriah the Hittite to be your wife" (2 Samuel 12:10). Nathan continued with God's judgment on David. "Behold, I will raise up adversity against you from your own house; and I will take your wives before your eyes and give them to your neighbor, and he shall lie with your wives in the sight of this sun. For you did it secretly, but I will do this thing before all Israel, before the sun" (2 Samuel 12:11, 12).

David would experience the expected consequence of sin as it works itself out in the life of the offender. Paul warned the Galatians, "Do not be deceived, God is not mocked; for whatever a man sows, that he will also reap. For he who sows to his flesh will of the flesh reap corruption, but he who sows to the Spirit will of the Spirit reap everlasting life" (Galatians 6:7, 8). The seed of sin David had sown would now begin producing its undesirable fruit in his life.

GREAT LEADERS NEED COURAGEOUS PEOPLE WHO WILL HOLD THEM ACCOUNTABLE FOR THEIR ACTIONS

A PRAYER OF REPENTANCE

While righteousness and justice are among the attributes of God, His judicial acts are often exercised with the goal of turning the hearts of His people back to Him. In this case, the pronouncement of His judgment had its desired effect. The king who had been silently agonizing over his sin for months now publicly acknowledged his guilt. Turning to Nathan, David confessed, "I have sinned against the LORD" (2 Samuel 12:13).

Six words hardly seem enough to undo all the damage King David had caused, but they were enough to deal with the problem that existed in his relationship with God. In response to David's confession of sin, Nathan shared a different message from God. "The LORD has also put away your sin; you shall not die" (2 Samuel 12:13).

The few words with which David expressed his repentance to Nathan were expanded in a psalm David wrote around this time to express his repentance before God. He cried out to God for mercy in prayer saying, "Have mercy upon me, O God, according to Your loving kindness; according to the multitude of your tender mercies, blot out my transgression. Wash me thoroughly from my iniquity, and cleanse me from my sin" (Psalm 51:1, 2).

Some in David's situation would be more distraught over being caught than about the sin that had been committed. Others might whine that God's judgment of their sin was too severe. This was not at all David's concern. He was thoroughly honest in acknowledging his sin and its offensiveness to God. "For I acknowledge my transgressions, and my sin is always before me. Against You, You only, have I sinned, and done this evil in Your sight – that You may be found just when You speak, and blameless when You judge" (Psalm 51:3, 4).

Throughout his prayer of repentance, David asked God to deal with his sin problem severely. Viewing sin as an infection that threatened to destroy him, he cried out, "Purge me with hyssop" (Psalm 51:7). The leaves of the hyssop are a natural host to the penicillin mold and were used as a natural medicine to cure the sick. As he thought of the filth of sin in his life, he prayed, "Wash me, and I shall be whiter than snow" (Psalm 51:7). He asked God to restore the physical damage caused by this sin in his life (Psalm 51:8) and to "blot out" that which was so offensive to God (Psalm 51:9). He called on God to transform his evil heart into a clean heart (Psalm 51:10) and pled with God not to remove His Holy Spirit from him (Psalm 51:11). "Restore to me the joy of Your salvation, and uphold me by Your generous Spirit" (Psalm 51:12).

He knew the path of sin he had traveled began when he failed to fulfill his responsibility as king to lead his troops into battle. If God would forgive him, David was prepared to renew his commitment to serve God wholeheartedly. "Then I will teach transgressors Your ways, and sinners shall be converted to You," he promised (Psalm 51:13). Not only would he serve God as a witness, he would also serve God with his worship. "Deliver me from the guilt of bloodshed, O God, the God of my salvation, and my tongue shall sing aloud of Your righteousness" (Psalm 31:14).

GREAT LEADERS ACKNOWLEDGE AND DEAL WITH THEIR FAILURE

A CHILD'S DEATH

Although God had forgiven David, the natural consequences of his sin would continue to impact the king for years to come. In his rage, David had pronounced a judgment consistent with the principles laid out in the law of God. A thief who stole a sheep was required by law to repay all he had stolen four-fold (Exodus 22:1). In the context of Nathan's parable, David was the rich man who had stolen another man's sheep. In his plot to conceal that sin, David had stolen the life of Uriah the Hittite. The debt he incurred in that act would be paid with the lives of four of David's sons.

The first installment on this payment would be paid in a week. Nathan explained, "Because by this deed you have given great occasion to the enemies of the LORD to blaspheme, the child also who is born to you shall surely die" (2 Samuel 12:14). It was not long at all before a messenger arrived to inform the king that his baby was sick.

David knew he was responsible for his son's condition and cried out to God desperately, hoping for a reprieve. For a week, his prayer was so intense that he abstained from eating, even when his servants brought him food. At night he stretched himself out on the ground, continuing to plead to God for the life of his son. But this judicial decision would be executed and as the week drew to a close, the child died.

When David learned of the child's death, he cleaned himself up, went to the Tabernacle to worship God, and then returned home to break his fast with a meal. His behavior seemed unusual to those closest to him. News of the death of a child marked the beginning of a period of grief, sometimes involving fasting, for most parents. But David's perspective was different. He explained, "While the child was alive, I fasted and wept; for I said, 'Who can tell whether the LORD will be gracious to me, that the child may live?' But now he is dead; why should I fast? Can I bring him back again? I shall go to him, but he shall not return to me" (2 Samuel 12:22, 23). David's hope of a reunion after death overcame his natural tendency to grieve.

GREAT LEADERS LIVE WITH THE CONSEQUENCES OF THEIR FAILURE

A SEASON OF HOPE

Typically, mothers find it harder to deal with the death of a child than fathers. David's hope gave him the resources he needed to comfort Bathsheba. The child that had died had been the result of an illegitimate and immoral relationship. As David ministered to his wife, they began building the kind of emotional bonds they had not taken time to build earlier. This deeper relationship between the king and his queen became the basis of a richer physical relation within the covenant of marriage. It was not long before Bathsheba once again announced she was pregnant.

Bathsheba's first announcement had caused fear and panic in the palace as David looked for a way to cover his sin. This announcement was a cause for great rejoicing and celebration. The son that was born received three names from three different sources. He is best known by the name his father gave him, Solomon. Nathan the prophet named the child Jedidiah, meaning, "beloved of the LORD." In light of the death of their previous child, David and Bathsheba may have feared for the health of their new son. Nathan acted on behalf of God to assure David his sins had been forgiven and that God loved this son.

But the child's mother apparently gave Solomon a third name. Perhaps it was a pet name she used as she interacted with her son. Regardless, even when he would someday be king, she would always think of him as her Lemuel. On at least one occasion,

Solomon revealed Bathsheba's name for him when he recorded some of the things "his mother taught him" (Proverbs 31:1).

What could an adulteress, who many would hold responsible for David's darkest hours, ever teach her son? Among other things, she taught him what God had apparently taught her and David during this most difficult time. "Do not give your strength to women, nor your ways to that which destroys kings" (Proverbs 31:3). Someday, Solomon would wield the power of his father David. When that day came, she prayed her son would not abuse it. "Open your mouth for the speechless, in the cause of all who are appointed to die. Open your mouth, judge righteously, and plead the cause of the poor and needy" (Proverbs 31:8, 9).

While the beginning of their relationship did much to discredit the reputations of both David and Bathsheba, the birth of Solomon was God's means of telling the couple He was still interested in using them for His glory. No doubt there were things they hoped their son would never learn, but the process of dealing with their sin had changed them. And what a change it made! Who would have thought that the adulteress would be the subject of her son's great poem on the virtuous wife (Proverbs 31:10-31)?

GREAT LEADERS CAN BE GREAT AGAIN

AMNON'S SIN

Sometimes, the things parents teach their children are not the things they intend to teach their children. Although David and Bathsheba had dealt with their sin and been forgiven, they had also, by example, taught David's sons a behavioral pattern that would be hard to reverse. Unfortunately, the pattern was quickly followed in the royal family.

David had married several wives and fathered children by most of them. In polygamous societies, wisdom dictates that a man provides a separate home for each wife and her children. Although the children of the same father all belong to the extended family, a sense of separateness exists between the siblings of different wives. They become more like cousins than brothers and sisters. This appears to have also been David's practice in the management of his household.

One of David's sons, Amnon, secretly loved one of his sisters, Tamar. He became so lovesick over her that he was not eating well and began losing weight. When Amnon's cousin Jonadab asked what was wrong, Amnon confided in him about his secret love. Jonadab, who did not possess a very noble character, developed a plan to help his cousin get what he wanted. All Amnon had to do was feign an illness and ask David to assign Tamar to be his nurse.

Amnon followed Jonadab's advice and soon Tamar was preparing meals for him to help him recover from his sickness. Amnon arranged for Tamar to be alone with him in the house and asked her to bring the food to him in bed. Not realizing she was in danger, the request to bring nourishing food to her brother in his sick bed did not seem unreasonable. But she had not been there long before she discovered that it was not food that interested him most.

When Amnon invited his sister to join him in bed, Tamar resisted. The kind of incestuous act her brother was suggesting was against everything she had been taught. "Do not force me, for no such thing should be done in Israel. Do not do this disgraceful thing!" she pleaded (2 Samuel 13:12). She explained she could not live with the shame and he would be perceived as a fool if he committed this act. But Amnon had already made his decision. "He would not heed her voice; and being stronger than she, he forced her and lay with her" (2 Samuel 13:14).

Amnon found no fulfillment in the rape of his sister. In contrast, his action destroyed the feelings he had previously held for her. "Then Amnon hated her exceedingly, so that the hatred with which he hated her was greater than the love with which he had loved her" (2 Samuel 13:15). After humiliating her in his bed, he sent her away and instructed his servants to bolt the door behind her as she left. He wanted nothing more to do with her.

GREAT LEADERS LEAD BY EXAMPLE, EVEN WHEN THE EXAMPLE IS NEGATIVE

TAMAR'S REVENGE

Devastated at being raped by her own brother, Tamar tore her brightly colored dress and covered herself in ashes. As she left Amnon's house, she buried her head in her hands and wept in anguish. Such actions were the usual expression of mourning or grief. It was not long before others who loved her figured out what had happened.

The first to notice was Tamar's brother Absalom. It was common knowledge that Amnon had requested Tamar to nurse him back to health. As Absalom saw his distraught sister leaving Amnon's house, he did not have to ask what had taken place. Concerned for his sister's welfare, he found room in his own home for her to live and work through the grieving process away from the public. But Absalom had more in mind than simply caring for his sister.

News of what happened also reached David. "When King David heard of all these things, he was very angry" (2 Samuel 13:21). But his anger was apparently not channeled into specific action to deal with the situation in his own home. Perhaps the anger he felt was anger at himself for what he had taught his son by example. Regardless, David's failure to act gave opportunity for others to seek justice for Tamar.

Absalom was willing to act but realized he would probably have only one opportunity to exact revenge. Patiently, he waited for that chance. Two years later, the opportunity came. He had flocks in Baal Hazor that needed shearing, which usually involved friends and family working and celebrating together. If he could get Amnon to join them, they would be far from Jerusalem and Absalom could take Tamar's revenge and escape the wrath of others in the family.

Just as Amnon had enlisted David's help in his scheme, so Absalom urged his father to let Amnon join him for the sheep shearing festival. Unaware of Absalom's intentions, David agreed. As they made their way to Baal Hazor, Absalom conducted himself in such a way that Amnon never suspected any problem. But the plot had already been devised before they left Jerusalem.

Absalom had instructed his servants to wait for orders to kill Amnon when he was drunk. He had waited two years for this moment and did not want anything to go wrong. He himself would give the order to act. And when he saw his brother overcome with the effects of the wine he was drinking, Absalom gave the order. "Then the servants of Absalom did to Amnon as Absalom had commanded" (2 Samuel 13:29).

Initially, Absalom's motive was not apparent. Other members of the royal family who witnessed the act assumed that Absalom was attempting to eliminate other potential heirs to the throne, and they ran for their lives. When the initial account of Absalom's actions reached David, it was wrongly reported that Absalom had killed all his brothers. Ironically, it was Jonadab, Amnon's friend who had been indirectly involved in the rape of Tamar, who reported what really happened and why. As for Absalom, he sought and found refuge in Geshur. It would be three years before he would return home.

GREAT LEADERS FACE MORE COMPLEX PROBLEMS WHEN THEY FAIL TO ADDRESS THE SIMPLER ONES

CHAPTER ELEVEN

WHEN CRITICS SEEM TO APPEAR FROM NOWHERE

2 Samuel 14:1-20:26; Psalms 3; 63

When he learned of Amnon's death, David began mourning. He was relieved to learn that only one son and not all his sons had been killed by Absalom, but that did not take away the pain of losing a child. Even knowing that Amnon's death had been a revenge killing, payment for his rape of Tamar, did not ease the pain. "David mourned for his son every day" (2 Samuel 13:37).

Absalom apparently did not expect this response from his father. David had done nothing to address the rape of his own daughter. Absalom's actions to protect the family honor were in keeping with the cultural practices of that day. In some families he might have been honored for his actions. He certainly had not counted on David mourning the loss of Amnon.

In light of David's response, Absalom went into a self-declared exile for three years. During that time, resentment began growing in him toward his father. David recovered from the loss of his son Amnon, but did nothing to welcome Absalom back. Down deep, he longed to see Absalom again, but the longer he waited to extend an offer of peace, the harder it became to do so.

Fortunately, Joab knew his king well enough to discern what

was going on. He also knew it was not his place to tell his king what to do. Still, something had to be done to reconcile the two men. He had always assumed that Absalom would someday succeed his father as king. If he could reconcile the two men now, the eventual transition of power would be smoother and his role in the kingdom would be secure in the next reign.

GREAT LEADERS SURROUND THEMSELVES WITH DISCERNING FOLLOWERS

THE WOMAN OF TEKOA

Joab knew of a woman living in Tekoa who could help him accomplish his goal. Her wisdom was legendary in her community and with the right coaching she could effectively communicate what David needed to hear. He contacted her and enlisted her aid. He told her she would be speaking to the king but that he did not want her to prepare herself as she might normally prepare to enter the presence of royalty. Instead, he instructed her, "Please pretend to be a mourner, and put on mourning apparel; do not anoint yourself with oil, but act like a woman who has been mourning a long time for the dead" (2 Samuel 14:2).

Under Joab's direction, the woman made her way to see David. The king was the final arbitrator in legal matters so it was not difficult to gain an audience with the king if there was an important matter to resolve. When she came to present her case, she told a story that Joab had prepared and appealed for David's help.

According to the woman, she was a widow and mother of two sons. She claimed her two boys had gotten into a fight and one had killed the other. When news of the murder reached others in the extended family, they demanded that she surrender her other son to be executed for his crime. She feared that if she lost that son, she would be left with no one to protect her and provide for her needs. When David heard the woman's case, he sympathized with her situation. He agreed to issue the order that her son be protected so as to care for his mother. Once David announced his decision, the woman pressed the matter further and received several assurances that the son would not be judged for his crime. She then had only one more thing to say.

"Why then have you schemed such a thing against the people of God?" she asked. "For the king speaks this thing as one who is guilty, in that the king does not bring his banished one home again" (2 Samuel 14:13). She pointed out that the same logic David used to address her case demanded that he reconcile with Absalom and bring him back to Jerusalem. The woman was articulate in presenting her case and there was little David could do to defend himself.

As the final argument was being presented to him, David recognized the hand of Joab behind this plot. When he asked the woman directly about Joab's involvement, she acknowledged his part and defended him, claiming it was still the right thing to do. Part of David was always suspect of Joab's loyalty and it was clear that he had been deceived by the woman standing before him. Still, she was right. Turning to Joab, he said, "All right, I have granted this thing. Go, therefore, bring back the young man Absalom" (2 Samuel 14:21).

GREAT LEADERS RESPOND TO WISE REBUKE REGARDLESS OF ITS SOURCE

ABSALOM'S TREASON

Although David agreed that Absalom could return to Jerusalem, he refused to meet his son personally. For the next two years, he lived as a crown prince in the royal city with his family. He had three sons and a daughter, each of whom was as physically attractive as their father. But the fact that he had not seen his father in over five years began to wear on him. Because Joab had been successful in getting him back to Jerusalem, he sent word to Joab to meet with him.

When Joab got Absalom's message, he knew he was in a difficult position. He knew exactly what Absalom wanted even before they met. He also knew that David had stubbornly refused to meet with his son over the past five years and had only reluctantly agreed to allow Absalom to return two years earlier, with the condition that they never meet. If Joab met with Absalom, he knew he would be asked to set up a meeting that may never take place. Therefore, he ignored the message from the crown prince and did nothing. When Absalom sent a subsequent request for a meeting, he continued to ignore the appeal.

Tired of being ignored, Absalom devised another way of getting Joab's attention. He ordered his men to set fire to a barley field belonging to Joab that was adjacent to his property. Barley was an important feed crop that Joab depended upon to feed his livestock. The loss of this field would quickly catch his attention. Also, it would not take long to discover the source of the arson. As Absalom had planned, Joab was soon at his door to meet.

When Joab charged Absalom with burning his field and asked why, Absalom reminded him that he had been ignoring his requests for a meeting. He noted that he was no better off in Jerusalem than he had been in exile, since he could not meet with his own father. Joab could no longer ignore the issue. He left Absalom and met with David to bring about reconciliation. When David agreed, Absalom came to the palace and humbled himself before his father. David responded by embracing his son and kissing him as Middle Eastern men greeted one another as friends. The relationship appeared to be restored after five stressful years.

However, bitterness was deeply rooted in Absalom's heart. He was looking for revenge for the wrongs he perceived his father had committed against him. But just as he had waited patiently for the right moment to trap his brother Amnon, so he would again wait patiently until he was strong enough to take on his father. The feigned kiss in the palace was just part of the plot. It would now give him access to the circles of power he needed to exploit if he hoped to win popular support for his undeclared plan.

Absalom began building a small armed force around him, including horses, chariots and bodyguards. The action was unlikely to arouse suspicion as many loyal leaders in David's army had troops directly accountable to them. Further, as the crown prince, it was expected that he would have certain troops assigned to protect him and would need to learn how to lead soldiers as part of his training to be king.

Absalom began getting up early to meet people at the gate as they congregated to try their cases. He would arrive before the judges arrived and talk with those who were gathered there. As he listened to people from across the country, he assured them they had a strong case and lamented the fact that there were so few judges and there was nothing he could do to resolve their problem. He knew people resented waiting long hours to have their case heard and he let them believe that he wanted to help them but could not as long as he was only a crown prince. Absalom's plan worked and before long his popularity throughout the land was greater than his father's.

With things now coming together as he planned, Absalom met with David and asked for permission to travel with others to Hebron. He claimed he needed to fulfill a vow he had made when he had been in exile in Syria, but failed to tell his father that the vow had been his own, to someday take the kingdom from his father. Assuming Absalom was going to fulfill a religious vow, David urged him to go in peace.

As Absalom prepared for his journey, he sent messengers to the many contacts he had developed throughout the kingdom and invited them to his coronation in Hebron. He was careful to hide the true purpose of the trip from many of those who traveled with him. As he traveled to Hebron and then spent several days there offering sacrifices, the size of the conspiracy grew significantly. Before long, the crowds in Hebron were so large that Absalom's intent could no longer be hidden. Soon a messenger arrived in Jerusalem bearing a heart-wrenching message for David. "The hearts of the people are with Absalom" (2 Samuel 15:13).

GREAT LEADERS RISK BETRAYAL FROM THOSE WHO ARE CLOSEST TO THEM

DAVID'S ESCAPE

The crisis that had arisen was unexpected in the palace. As reports arrived detailing the size of Absalom's following and listing various key individuals who had aligned with this coup, it was obvious that David was in real danger. Although Jerusalem was located in a strategic place for defensive purposes, he realized that Absalom had often heard the story from both him and Joab how Jerusalem had been conquered to become the city of David. He could not run the risk of staying in the royal city and waiting for Absalom's armed invasion.

David led his loyal supporters out of the city. Once he was through the city gate, he paused to let others pass and took notice of those who were taking a stand with him. One of the first groups he noticed were a band of old soldiers, the six hundred men who had been under his command since his escape from Gath. As they passed by, they were a reminder of the many victories they had shared together in battle. They were also a reminder of the years they had spent in the wilderness during the reign of Saul, and how God had provided for them then.

David was surprised to see Ittai the Gittite among the soldiers. Ittai had only recently pledged his loyalty to David and they had little history together. Many mercenaries in similar circumstances would quickly cut their losses and look for a stronger, more secure leader to support. But Ittai's pledge of loyalty had been sincere and he continued to believe in David's leadership in spite of the circumstances.

The priests and Levites were also among those who remained loyal to David. They demonstrated this loyalty by marching out of the city bearing the Ark of the Covenant. David knew God had chosen Jerusalem as the worship center of Israel and was not comfortable with the idea of taking the ark into the wilderness. He ordered the men to return it to the Tabernacle where it belonged.

Having been encouraged by the loyalty of his men and Ittai's faith in him, his own faith in God was strengthened. "If I find favor in the eyes of the LORD, He will bring me back and show me both it, and His dwelling place," David explained (2 Samuel 15:25).

Brokenhearted, David and his people wept as they made their way up the Mount of Olives. It was then he learned that one of his trusted counselors, Ahithophel, had joined Absalom's rebellion. David knew Absalom would receive wise counsel from Ahithophel and asked God to intervene. "O LORD, I pray, turn the counsel of Ahithophel into foolishness!" he prayed (2 Samuel 15:31). God's answer to this prayer arrived faster than David might have thought possible.

Another of David's counselors came running out of the city to join his king. Hushai the Archite was a wise counselor whose friendship with David was widely known. When he came to the king with his pledge of loyalty, David recognized that he could be more helpful if he remained in Jerusalem. David asked Hushai to feign defecting to Absalom and work undercover. He knew Absalom would welcome Hushai into his inner circle, where Hushai could be part of the decision-making process. He could then communicate information to the priests who would pass on the information to family members in David's camp. This would help David in two ways. He would have someone in Absalom's inner circle undermining the influence of Ahithophel and he would know what Absalom was planning to do before it happened.

GREAT LEADERS
MAINTAIN GREAT FLEXIBILITY
IN RESPONDING TO SITUATIONS

LIARS AND CRITICS

Among those who followed David out of Jerusalem was Ziba, the servant of Mephibosheth. When David saw Ziba, he looked for Mephibosheth but did not see him in the group. When he asked Ziba about Mephibosheth, the servant claimed he had remained in

Jerusalem, as he was sympathetic with Absalom's rebellion. David did not know that Ziba was lying and had left without his master, hoping to drive a wedge between David and Mephibosheth. Based on what he heard, David was deeply wounded by Mephibosheth's apparent betrayal. After all he had done for Jonathan's son, David expected his loyalty. What happened next would only rub salt in this wound.

As David descended through the valley of Kidron, the first town they passed was Bahurim. As Shimei saw the royal entourage pass by his hometown, he cursed David from the ridge and cast stones down on him. Committed to protecting their king, David's men gathered around him. While there was no real danger from Shimei's actions, this was public humiliation of David, and his men were deeply offended that their king was treated in such a way.

Shimei was a descendant of Saul and a natural enemy of David. In his accusation against David, he claimed the king had usurped the throne from the royal family and was being judged for that action. "The LORD has brought upon you all the blood of the house of Saul, in whose place you have reigned; and the LORD has delivered the kingdom into the hand of Absalom your son. So now you are caught in your own evil, because you are a bloodthirsty man!" (2 Samuel 16:8)

Shimei's deep-seated grudge meant that he would not be objective in his criticism of David. He blamed David for everything that was wrong in his life. If the kingdom had been passed on to one of Saul's heirs, Shimei would be enjoying the privileges of being part of the royal family. The extreme bitterness of his heart was revealed when he called David a son of Belial, or a rogue. This term is used throughout the Scriptures to describe one given over to drunkenness (1 Samuel 1:16), abuse of power (1 Samuel 2:12), idolatry (Deuteronomy 13:13), rebellion (1 Samuel 10:27) and sexual sin (Judges 19:22).

Those traveling with David wanted to silence Shimei. Abishai turned to his king and asked, "Why should this dead dog curse my lord the king? Please, let me go over and take off his head!" (2 Samuel 16:9). But David refused Abishai's request. "See how my son who came from my own body seeks my life. How much more now may this Benjamite?" David answered (2 Samuel 16:11). A critic from the ridge would not distract him. The way David felt at that moment, he was willing to concede that God may have even directed Shimei to speak on His behalf.

GREAT LEADERS ARE NOT DISTRACTED FROM MAJOR PROBLEMS BY MINOR CONCERNS

HUSHAI'S INTERVENTION

When Absalom arrived in Jerusalem, he immediately challenged Hushai's loyalty. He knew the advisor had supported his father for many years. Hushai argued that it was his responsibility to serve Israel's king, regardless of who that king might be. He added that he personally preferred to serve the previous king's son rather than someone else. Convinced by Hushai's logic, Absalom welcomed him into his inner circle. He then turned to Ahithophel to discuss their next course of action.

Ahithophel advised Absalom that it was time to take action that would alienate David and his followers and strengthen the resolve of his own followers. When David left Jerusalem, he had left ten concubines behind to maintain the palace until he returned. As conquering kings often incorporated a previous king's harem into his own, Absalom was advised to take the concubines for himself. Based on this advice, Absalom had his tent pitched on the palace roof so everyone in the city could see him take his father's concubines into his own tent.

Next, Ahithophel advised an immediate attack on David and offered to lead it himself. "Now let me choose twelve thousand men, and I will arise and pursue David tonight. I will come upon him while he is weary and weak, and make him afraid. And all the people who are with him will flee, and I will strike only the king. Then I will bring back all the people to you. When all return except the man whom you seek, all the people will be at peace" (2 Samuel 17:1-3).

Ahithophel's counsel made sense to Absalom and won the support of the elders of Israel who were backing Absalom. No one wanted a drawn out conflict between father and son, and this sounded like the quickest way to resolve the situation with minimal loss of life. But before agreeing to this course of action, Absalom called on Hushai for his input.

Hushai knew that everything Ahithophel had said would be advantageous to Absalom's cause, but he was there to advance David's cause. David needed time to get organized and prepare to defend himself. Therefore, Hushai reminded Absalom that his father was both an experienced soldier and a desperate man; this combination made him extremely dangerous. He suggested David had probably already secured himself and could do serious damage to a small attack group. If that happened, Hushai explained, the people would conclude, "There is a slaughter among the people who follow Absalom" (2 Samuel 17:9).

At this fragile time of establishing Absalom's claim to the throne, that kind of bad press would be devastating to morale. Hushai argued, "Even he who is valiant, whose heart is like the heart of a lion, will melt completely. For all Israel knows that your father is a mighty man, and those who are with him are valiant. Therefore I advise that all Israel be fully gathered to you, from Dan to Beersheba, like the sand that is by the sea for multitude, and that you go to battle in person" (2 Samuel 17:10, 11). He urged Absalom to consolidate his strength, forfeiting the element of surprise to attack with overwhelming force.

God used Hushai's counsel to answer David's prayer. Absalom and the elders of Israel were convinced by Hushai's logic and believed it to be better advice than Ahithophel's had been. They did not realize that this new plan meant forfeiting the only real advantage they had and would place their new king at personal risk in the final conflict. When Ahithophel realized his advice had been rejected, he left Jerusalem to return home. Frustrated by his failure to see David killed, he committed suicide.

Hushai then passed on what he knew to Zadok and Abiathar, knowing they would get word to David. It would not seem out of place for Hushai to be seen with the priests, as they were Israel's religious leaders. Anyone who witnessed the meeting would assume the topic of conversation was religious rather than political.

A young boy saw the messengers who would carry the message to David and reported their presence to Absalom. Absalom quickly sent troops to capture the men, but they returned empty handed. A woman had hidden the messengers and then sent Absalom's men looking for them in a different direction. When the troops returned to Jerusalem, the messengers completed their assignment and shared the message with David.

GREAT LEADERS DEPEND UPON THE LOYALTY OF THEIR CLOSEST ADVISORS

UNEXPECTED ENCOURAGEMENT

Hushai advised David to create some distance between himself and Absalom by crossing the Jordan and warned David about Ahithophel's advice. Although his advice was accepted above Ahithophel's, Hushai could not be certain that Absalom would not change his mind again. By morning, David and his followers were safely across the Jordan River and on their way to Mahanaim, his capital in exile.

When David crossed the Jordan River, Absalom was drawn out of Jerusalem and established his battle camp in Gilead. But Absalom was not the only one on the move. Shobi, Machir and Barzillai, leaders of people who had benefited under David's reign, sent supplies to David in Mahanaim to encourage him. They sent "beds and basins, earthen vessels and wheat, barley and flour, parched grain and beans, lentils and parched seeds, honey and curds, sheep and cheese of the herd, for David and the people who were with him to eat" (2 Samuel 17:28, 29).

These leaders knew that David and his followers had left Jerusalem quickly. They concluded that the people had not had time to pack the supplies they needed in their haste to flee to freedom. Their practical humanitarian aid was a means by which they could thank David for his past generosity toward them. Their actions encouraged David to realize that the whole world was not against him, even though it felt like it at the time.

GREAT LEADERS ARE REMEMBERED AND REWARDED FOR THEIR ACTS OF KINDNESS

TRUSTING GOD WHEN HOPE IS ALMOST GONE

David struggled in the midst of this situation with Absalom. Because the coup had arisen from within his own family, the problem he faced seemed larger that it probably was. In a psalm written during this season of his life, David cried out to God, "LORD, how they have increased who trouble me! Many are they who rise up against me. Many are they who say of me, 'There is no help for him in God'" (Psalm 3:1, 2).

Despite the claims of David's enemies, he continued trusting in God. "But You, O LORD, are a shield for me, My glory and the One who lifts up my head" (Psalm 3:3). He knew God was his defender and called upon him for aid. He did so with full confidence that God heard his prayer and would answer it.

Sometimes, good sleep is enough to change one's perspective. David was secure in Mahanaim and encouraged by the acts of kindness he had received. "I lay down and slept; I awoke, for the LORD sustained me," he wrote. "Therefore I will not be afraid of ten thousands of people who have set themselves against me all around" (Psalm 3:5, 6).

GREAT LEADERS SEE BEYOND DARK TIMES TO BRIGHT NEW DAYS

David knew that God had called him to be Israel's king and grew increasingly more confident that he would return to his throne in Jerusalem. He remembered previous occasions when God had "struck all my enemies on the cheekbone" and "broken the teeth of the ungodly" (Psalm 3:7). What God had done in the past could be repeated again. Confident of ultimate success, he declared, "But the king shall rejoice in God; everyone who swears by Him shall glory; but the mouth of those who speak lies shall be stopped" (Psalm 63:11).

GREAT LEADERS ARE CONFIDENT OF GOD'S INTEREST IN THEIR SUCCESS

KEEPING A FOCUS IN FOGGY CONDITIONS

Not everyone who watched David's situation was as convinced as David was of his ultimate success. Most would have concluded that things would turn out differently based on the way they appeared. But David understood that circumstances did not dictate failure or success. They were merely opportunities for God to work through.

David maintained this perspective on his situation through the daily discipline of seeking God early in the day. "O God, You are my God; early will I seek You; my soul thirsts for You; my flesh longs for You in a dry and thirsty land where there is no water" (Psalm 63:1). By focusing his heart and mind on God at the beginning of each day, he was sensitive to the hand of God working throughout the day.

But morning was not the only time David made God his focus, "When I remember You on my bed, I meditate on You in the night watches" (Psalm 63:6). As he rested his head and whenever he awoke during the night, David took time to remember the good things God had recently done for him. This discipline helped him maintain a positive mental attitude in the midst of his trying situation.

GREAT LEADERS FOCUS THEIR THOUGHTS TO MAINTAIN A POSITIVE MENTAL ATTITUDE

The discipline of looking to God and recognizing His hand at work in his life led David into an even deeper commitment to God. Just as abandoning spiritual disciplines like Bible study and prayer cause Christians to backslide even further, so seeking God draws the people of God to seek Him more. "Because You have been my help, therefore in the shadow of Your wings I will rejoice. My soul follows close behind You; Your right hand upholds me" (Psalm 62:7, 8).

THE DEATH OF ABSALOM

Although danger was real, David's faith in God gave him a confidence his own son could not understand. Absalom placed his confidence in the wide support base he had established. David placed his confidence in God. That alone would determine the outcome of this conflict.

David divided his troops into three groups under the leadership of Joab, Abishai and Ittai. When he announced that he would also be involved, aligning himself with different groups at different times in what he expected might be a long conflict, his people objected. He was the reason they were resisting Absalom and they did not think he should risk being killed in battle. The king recognized their wisdom and reluctantly entrusted the inevitable conflict to his three chosen generals.

Despite all Absalom had done to harm David, David remained reluctant to harm his son. Before his generals went out to meet the rebel force, he pleaded with them, "Deal gently for my sake with the young man Absalom" (2 Samuel 18:5). In the midst of the most serious political crisis of his career, he never stopped caring for Absalom as his son, hoping they could be reconciled.

The battle took place in the forest of Ephraim and went decidedly in David's favor. Twenty thousand in Absalom's army fell in battle and it was not long before Absalom himself was in conflict with David's soldiers. In a desperate attempt to retreat to safety, Absalom rode his mule back toward his base camp. In the process, his long thick hair got caught in the branches of the trees and his mule ran off without him.

When David's soldiers saw Absalom hanging helpless in the tree, they reported the news to Joab expecting that he would take Absalom back to David. Joab was infuriated with the report. "You just saw him!" he exclaimed. "And why did you not strike him there to the ground? I would have given you ten shekels of silver and a belt" (2 Samuel 18:11). His men reminded Joab of David's command not to harm Absalom, but Joab was not interested in what they said. "I cannot linger with you?" he complained (2 Samuel 18:14). Then he grabbed three spears himself and thrust them through Absalom's heart. Following their leaders example, ten of Joab's armor bearers also struck the corpse.

With Absalom dead and his army dead or scattered, Joab sounded the trumpet call for victory. He had the body of Absalom cut down and thrown into a deep pit in the forest. Then rocks were piled into the pit. From the site of Absalom's fall, messengers were sent to report the news to David. When David heard the news of Absalom's death, his elation over the victory turned to mourning over his son. "O my son Absalom – my son, my son Absalom – if only I had died in your place! O Absalom my son, my son!" he cried (2 Samuel 18:33).

GREAT LEADERS CARE FOR THEIR ADVERSARIES

THE RETURN TO JERUSALEM

There was not much of a victory celebration that day. Everyone knew how deeply grieved David was and out of respect for their king, they grieved with him. "And the people stole back into the city that day, as people who are ashamed steal away when they flee in battle" (2 Samuel 19:3). When Joab realized what was happening, he went to David and rebuked him for his response. He claimed David's personal grief was affecting his people negatively at a time when they ought to rejoice. Although he still grieved deeply over his son, David realized he had to send a signal to his people that he was once again in control of the kingdom. Setting his personal feelings aside, he made his way to the city gate to judge cases brought before him. This act gave his followers a sense that things were beginning to return to normal.

But things were not as they had been! Israel had been deeply divided by Absalom's attempted coup. Some had not supported Absalom until they heard that David had left Jerusalem. Others were confused with the news of Absalom's death. They thought he would overcome in the conflict and rule as king. In the midst of this, many were confused over the failure of Israel's leaders to lead in this moment of crisis. They had supported Absalom in his rebellion, and were now among the last to welcome David back to his rightful place as Israel's king.

When the invitation for David to return finally came, there were still many bitter feelings among the people. Some of those feelings were revealed when David met Shimei, who had come among others to welcome David back. Shimei humbled himself before David and apologized for his previous actions. But Abishai was not convinced he should be forgiven. Once again he argued for Shimei's execution, but once again David intervened. Just as he had to set aside his personal feelings for the good of the nation in the death of Absalom, now it was time for Israel to do the same. He reminded those present that it was a day to celebrate his restoration to the throne, not a day to seek revenge on others.

Throughout the day, David extended mercy to those he met. It was not until he arrived back in Jerusalem that he learned what really happened with Mephibosheth when he left. He had been betrayed by his servant, and he chose to demonstrate his loyalty to David by refusing to maintain his hygiene or personal grooming until David returned. When they met, David could see and smell that Mephibosheth had remained loyal throughout the crisis despite his disability.

David also took time to reward Barzillai for his kindness and care during David's stay at Mahanaim. While Barzillai appreciated David's gesture, he declined the favor offered. Instead, the kindness shown to Barzillai was passed on to his son Chimham, who became part of David's inner circle.

GREAT LEADERS WISELY BALANCE JUSTICE AND MERCY

THE REBELLION OF SHEBA

The leaders of Judah had been proactive in welcoming David home. The division among the tribes was so deep that even this act became a source of conflict. Israel complained that Judah had no right to welcome David without representatives from their tribes. In fact, Israel's leaders had been reluctant to welcome David back until pressure had been placed on them. Although the dispute was resolved, an uneasy tension continued to exist in Israel.

Like many of his fellow Benjamites, Sheba had long opposed David's rule over Israel. Sensing the mood of the nation and perceiving David as weakened due to his conflict with Absalom, he seized the opportunity to lead his own rebellion. He successfully gained much of Israel's support with the statement, "We have no share in David, nor do we have inheritance in the son of Jesse: Every man to his tents, O Israel!" (2 Samuel 20:1). He gathered a strong following by associating himself with a widely held feeling of discontent.

GREAT LEADERS ARE CHALLENGED WHEN THEY ARE PERCEIVED AS WEAK

David recognized that this threat of rebellion was even more serious than that of Absalom. Turning to Amasa, he ordered him to assemble Judah's army within three days to mount an offensive. But Amasa failed to complete the task within the three days. David ordered Abishai to take all the troops they had and pursue Sheba before he got settled, as it had been Absalom's delay in attacking David that had enabled him to win that conflict.

Abishai and Joab led David's men into the conflict. En route Joab met Amasa and approached him to greet him. Not suspecting anything, Amasa was not aware of the weapon in Joab's hand until it sliced open his stomach so wide his entrails fell out to the ground. Leaving Amasa on the ground to bleed, he then incorporated Amasa's troops into the force to attack Sheba.

They pursued Sheba until they trapped him in Abel of Beth Maachah. David's troops surrounded the city and began building a siege mound. It quickly became evident to the residents of the city there would be difficult days ahead. Hoping to avoid further problems, a wise woman in the city entered into negotiations with Joab. Invoking an ancient custom of the city, she suggested that Joab request what he really wanted and the city would comply without a battle. Joab claimed he had no desire to destroy the city but that he could not leave without Sheba.

"Watch," the woman answered. "His head will be thrown to you over the wall" (2 Samuel 20:21). She then met with the people and suggested they accept the deal she had negotiated. It did not take much to convince them. Sheba was decapitated and his head thrown from the wall toward Joab's camp. Once he had confirmed that it was Sheba's head, Joab led David's men back to Jerusalem.

CHAPTER TWELVE

WHEN IT IS TIME TO TURN OVER THE REINS

2 Samuel 21:1-23:7; 1 Kings 1:1-2:12; Psalms 18; 72

Having survived a series of rebellions, David was once again in control of the kingdom. Still, things were not the way they had been. He struggled with the loss of his son Absalom and the instability the kingdom had passed through. Thankfully his reorganization of the nation had established men he could rely on in key administrative roles. This new administrative structure would make it increasingly more difficult for men like Sheba to lead a successful rebellion against David or anyone else who would someday rule Israel. However, something was still not right.

Even when David had been fighting the threat from within the kingdom, he had been at peace with other nations bordering Israel. That state of peace continued after he again assumed the throne. Maintaining peace had been a key objective to help the nation develop its national economy. But despite the peace, the economy was not doing well. As he consulted with his advisors, David soon learned the reason. In an age when agriculture was a key indicator of economic prosperity, the country was experiencing a famine.

Nations in the Middle East were not unfamiliar with famines. Farmers in any nation reported good years and bad years on a regular basis. In the first year of the famine, most people probably assumed it was just one of the bad years that occurred from time to time. Some years, the rain would not come at all or would come at the wrong time for the crops grow. Or maybe it was one of those years when the insects swarmed out of nowhere. Sometimes, these things just happened. It would not be easy, but they knew they could get through it if they stayed focused.

Unfortunately, this time was different. The famine that year was followed by a famine the next year. Most of the stockpiles of grain had been used to survive last year's famine. Also, when sheep, goats and cattle were butchered, they were leaner and smaller than usual. Those who had hoped last year's famine would pass now began to worry. If they hadn't already been doing so, people throughout the land began calling on God for rain, or to eliminate the insect problem. The famine was a reminder of their dependence upon God.

When the spring rains again failed to come, it was clear there would be a third year of famine. By now, farmers had to use their seed to provide food for their families. Herds were being culled for meat and to make them more manageable under the new conditions in the fields. Shepherds knew it would take years to rebuild the flocks to their previous size. Knowing there was little he could do as king to alleviate the situation, David joined others in calling out to God for divine intervention. He could not understand why the nation's prayers had not already been answered. It was not long before he found out.

JUSTICE FOR THE GIBEONITES

"It is because of Saul and his bloodthirsty house, because he killed the Gibeonites" (2 Samuel 21:1). This was God's explanation for three years of famine in Israel. Though he may not have known the exact nature of the crime, David must have suspected there was something wrong in the nation. Moses had warned Israel that the same God who blessed them would also curse them if their hearts wandered from Him. Famine was one of the most common expressions of this judgment.

The Gibeonites were not one of the tribes of Israel but had been largely assimilated into the culture. Their cities predated the cities of Israel and were not destroyed by Joshua because they had been proactive and formed a treaty with Israel before its army arrived at Gibeon. That action had alienated them from other tribal nations in the land, but placed them under Israel's protection.

Early in his reign, Saul violated this treaty in his defense of Jabesh Gilead. His attack against the Amorites had been severe and relentless. While it was necessary to defeat Nahash and his army to protect the people of Jabesh Gilead, Saul appears to have attacked other Amorite tribes at that time, including the Gibeonites. His unchecked zeal had caused great hardship to the Gibeonites and they had never been compensated for their loss.

The attempted genocide of a people was serious, and was the reason for Israel's present difficulties. Knowing the reconciliation of this issue was key to the restoration of God's blessing on Israel, David consulted with Gibeonite leaders, acknowledged Israel's wrongdoing in this matter, and asked them what would be an appropriate payment to correct this wrong. Under normal circumstances, a large monetary payment and the execution of a significant number of Israel's citizens would be requested.

The Gibeonites responded by making it clear they believed it was Saul and not the nation itself who was responsible for the previous action. They were not interested in getting rich off this situation and requested no financial payment. Further, they did not want to see innocent Israelites die to atone for the murder of innocent Gibeonites. Instead, they asked that seven of Saul's direct descendants be held accountable for the sins of their father and be executed.

David realized the Gibeonite request was both temperate and reasonable and quickly agreed. He ordered that seven men, direct descendants of Saul, be turned over to the Gibeonites. In giving the order, he remembered his own covenant with Jonathan to protect his family; all descendants of Jonathan were exempt from the selection process. By the time the barley was being harvested in Israel, the seven representative descendants of Saul lay dead in the field. It was not long after this that the rains returned and the people's prayers began to be answered again.

GREAT LEADERS SEEK TO CORRECT PAST WRONGS WITHOUT COMPROMISING PRESENT COMMITMENTS

TAKING ON GIANTS AGAIN

The famine had impacted more than Israel. It was not long before the Philistines once again decided to raid Israel, probably intending to loot the land's grain and livestock. When news of the invasion reached David in Jerusalem, he called his army together and led them into battle as he had done so many times before. But this time was different from before.

David was getting old and it was beginning to show physically. The hardships he had endured as a young man in exile, the stress of being in the heat of conflict, the emotional strain of domestic struggles, and the various diseases that had ravished his body had all left their mark. He was simply not as alert and agile as he had been in his younger years. Eventually, his deteriorating condition would leave him bedridden with circulation so poor there was nothing anyone could do to warm his body. While it had not yet come to this, David was not the strong man he had once been.

Like many men his age, David was aware he could not do everything he used to, but he was not quick to admit it. He seemed to feel that, if he could not fight as hard as he once had, he could fight smarter and still win. In the battle against the Philistines, it became obvious that his strategy did not work. As the battle wore on, he found himself getting tired. Before he knew it, he was in mortal combat with a Philistine giant, Ishbi-Benob. David's career as a soldier began when he had killed a Philistine giant. Now it looked like his life would end at the hand of another giant.

Fortunately, a soldier named Abishai saw the plight of his king before it was too late. Coming to David's rescue, he killed Ishbi-Benob and saved David's life. This was the last battle David would fight. When the battle was complete and being reviewed by David and his generals, his men insisted that the king let them fight on his behalf. "You shall go out no more with us to battle, lest you quench the lamp of Israel" (1 Samuel 21:17).

It must have been a difficult moment for the king to face, but he knew his men were right. His experience with the Philistine giant demonstrated that he was more of a liability than an asset on the battlefield. If he died in battle, it would demoralize Israel and be a morale boost for his enemies. He had appointed good men to lead his army. Now it was time to let them do their jobs.

In subsequent battles, the new policy proved effective. Not having to protect their king freed the army to concentrate on defeating the enemy. This resulted in clear victories over the Philistines and the deaths of three additional giants of Gath. Through the efforts of David and his men, Goliath and his four brothers were eliminated and no longer posed a threat to Israel.

GREAT LEADERS RECOGNIZE THEIR LIMITS AND MAKE NECESSARY ADJUSTMENTS

GIVING GLORY TO WHOM GLORY IS DUE

The demise of the giants of Gath was a cause for celebration. Though only five men, their enormous size had a demoralizing effect on Israel's army when they met the Philistines in battle. It was obvious now that they could be conquered, but it never seemed that way before. While various individuals had accomplished heroic efforts on the battlefield and were commended for those actions, David knew the real source of his victory came from God. He acknowledged the same in a psalm he wrote to celebrate his victory over his enemies.

"The LORD is my rock and my fortress and my deliverer; the God of my strength in whom I will trust; my shield and the horn of my salvation, my stronghold and my refuge; my Savior" (2 Samuel 22:2, 3). He acknowledged that God had saved him from the violence of others and declared, "I will call upon the LORD, who is worthy to be praised; so shall I be saved from my enemies" (2 Samuel 22:4).

Despite his reputation as a great military leader, David was not afraid to acknowledge his personal moments of weakness and dependence upon God in this personal hymn of praise. Describing several battlefield experiences, he wrote, "When the waves of death surrounded me, the floods of ungodliness made me afraid, the sorrows of sheol surrounded me; the snares of death confronted me, in my distress I called upon the LORD, and cried out to my God; he heard my voice from His temple, and my cry entered His ears" (2 Samuel 22:5-7).

GREAT LEADERS VIEW THEIR INFLUENCE AS A GIFT FROM GOD

ESTABLISHING A MEMORIAL

Although David's psalm was his personal expression of thanksgiving for all God had done on his behalf, he also understood that it would be of spiritual benefit to his people. Therefore, David incorporated this psalm into his collection of psalms to be used in Israel's corporate worship (Psalm 18). The title of this psalm specifies that it was written "on the day that the LORD delivered him from the hand of all his enemies and from the hand of Saul" (Title Psalm 18).

Throughout the psalm, David celebrates the incredible power of God as evidenced in various natural phenomena including storms, earthquakes and volcanic activity. He notes that this powerful God is also the one who took a personal interest in his life. While David had done his part on the battlefield, it is clear that he attributes all his personal success to God's action on his behalf. "You have delivered me from the strivings of the people; You have made me the head of the nations" (Psalm 18:43).

David was in his last days and would soon pass from the earth, but God would continue to live long after he was gone. "The LORD lives! Blessed be my Rock! Let the God of my salvation be exalted" (Psalm 18:46). For all God had done, he would return thanks to Him alone. This would be his personal response to God; beyond that, he wanted everyone to know how he felt about the situation. "Great deliverance He gives to His king, and shows mercy to His anointed, to David and his descendants forevermore" (Psalm 18:50).

GREAT LEADERS CONSIDER TRANSPARENCY TO BE A STRONG CHARACTERISTIC

ADONIJAH'S ATTEMPTED COUP

While some people are blessed with good health until the day they die, this was not David's lot in life. Those closest to the king tried to do what they could to make David's final days more comfortable, but nothing proved effective. For those who knew their king best and loved him, it was heart wrenching to watch the body of Israel's champion continue wasting away.

Among those who knew how truly poor David's health had become was his son Adonijah, the younger brother of the now deceased Absalom. Seeing the weak state of his father, he determined that now was the time to usurp the throne of his father and become Israel's next king. He gathered loyal horsemen and chariots around him and enlisted Joab and Abithar to support him in his plan. With Israel's military and religious leaders on his side, Adonijah was certain of success in taking the throne from a sick, bed-ridden old man.

During his lifetime, it was widely assumed that Absalom was the heir to the throne. Upon the death of Absalom, Adonijah considered himself next in line of succession. He must have suspected David would not support his claim. This explains why he did not involve his father in the plans for his coronation. Instead, he gathered around him those whom he knew were loyal to his cause and planned a banquet event at the oasis En-Rogel. In his well-orchestrated plan, he even had trumpeters and heralds to announce his ascension to the throne.

GREAT LEADERS ARE MOST VULNERABLE IN THEIR SEASONS OF WEAKNESS

NATHAN'S INTERVENTION

The problem with Adonijah's plans was that God had previously chosen Solomon as David's heir. This was known by those most loyal to David, including Nathan the prophet and David's own select mighty leaders. Adonijah was probably also aware of David's desire to have Solomon sit on his throne. "He did not invite Nathan the prophet, Benaiah, the mighty men, or Solomon his brother" to his coronation (1 Kings 1:10).

Adonijah's plot was already underway when Nathan learned of it. He knew he had to act quickly to stop the coronation from taking place. He contacted Bathsheba and urged her to go to David and tell him what was happening. Because of his poor health, he was not being consulted on affairs of state and was not aware of these plans. As Bathsheba concluded her report, Nathan himself arrived in the king's room to confirm the report. Under Old Testament law, all information had to be confirmed by two or three witnesses. The parallel statements of Bathsheba and Nathan were sufficient to convince David of what was transpiring.

There was little David could do at this late hour to prevent the coronation of Adonijah, but he could arrange the coronation of

Solomon in a manner that clarified David's position and undermined Adonijah's claim to the throne. He called Zadok the priest, Nathan the prophet, and Beniaiah, one of his most trusted soldiers. He ordered them to take Solomon to Gihon, a spring east of Jerusalem in the Kidron Valley, anoint him king and make a public announcement.

GREAT LEADERS MAKE GREAT DECISIONS WHEN FULLY INFORMED

THE CORONATION OF SOLOMON

David knew it was important that the public perceive Solomon's coronation to be superior to Adonijah's. Therefore, he insisted on including three actions in the process that would give Solomon greater credibility. First, on the trip to the spring and back to Jerusalem, Solomon was directed to ride on David's mule. People in the city had seen their king ride on this mule and would quickly identify with it. They would naturally assume the one riding it had the delegated authority of David.

Second, Solomon was to be publicly anointed by both Zadock and Nathan. Samuel had anointed David himself initially when he was first informed he would someday rule Israel. At that time, Samuel was serving the nation in both the office of priest and prophet. Solomon's coronation was to be like David's own call to ministry. This also declared that his claim to the throne was distinct from his brother's.

At the conclusion of the coronation, the men were directed to bring Solomon back to Jerusalem and have him sit in David's throne. If there was any question of David's loyalty, his invitation for Solomon to sit on the throne, the symbol of authority in the kingdom, certainly clarified the issue. While Adonijah and his followers celebrated his claim to the throne, Solomon was sitting on the throne making decisions with the full support of his father.

GREAT LEADERS COMMUNICATE STRONG MESSAGES THROUGH THEIR ACTIONS

As Adonijah and his followers were concluding their meal, they could hear the trumpets announcing Solomon's ascension to his father's throne. When Jonathan, the son of Abiathar the priest, announced what had taken place, "all the guests who were with Adonijah were afraid, and arose, and each one went his own way" (1 Kings 1:49). Adonijah found he was alone with no one to defend his claim to the throne. Understandably, "Adonijah was afraid of Solomon; so he arose, and went and took hold of the horns of the altar" (1 Kings 1:50).

When Solomon learned his brother had taken sanctuary in the Tabernacle, he sent word to him that he would not be executed but rather placed on probation. "If he proves himself a worthy man, not one hair of him shall fall to the earth, but if wickedness be found in him, he shall die" (1 Kings 1:52). Adonijah humbled himself before his brother, the new king, and was sent to his home. When he later proved that his profession of loyalty had been feigned, by again attempting to usurp the throne, he was executed.

HELPING A NEW KING

Solomon gave David no reason to regret his decision. As the days of his life were coming to an end, David met with his son one more time. He again urged Solomon to pursue God's agenda for the nation and remain loyal to Him. But he also took time to share with Solomon insight into matters crucial to his reign.

Over the years, David had acquired a keen insight into character, and his experiences with three individuals had made profound impressions on him. When he was gone, Solomon would have to deal with these three individuals without the benefit of David's history. David took time to warn his son that Joab and Shimei could not be trusted and should be watched carefully. He also pointed out that although Barzillai might not make the kind of positive first impression others made, he had proved himself faithful and Solomon should always keep him close.

GREAT LEADERS PASS ON THEIR INSIGHTS TO THEIR SUCCESSORS

DAVID'S FINAL STATEMENTS

As his life came to its inevitable end, David had a very clear sense that all the good he had accomplished was the result of God's call and blessing upon him. In his final recorded statement, he began with the words, "Thus says David the son of Jesse; thus says the man raised up on high, the anointed of the God of Jacob, and the sweet psalmist of Israel" (2 Samuel 23:1). Even in his last days, he never forgot where he came from and marveled that God had elevated him from his humble beginnings.

David had no personal sense of grandeur as he made this statement for the benefit of others who would follow him. His description of himself as "the anointed of the God of Jacob" hints at his awareness that he, like Jacob the Patriarch, had not always been all God meant him to be. If he was Israel's sweet psalmist, it was because God had been pleased to speak to him and to others through him (2 Samuel 23:2).

His forty years on the throne, along with his experience of being pursued by the former king, had given him a unique perspective on what was involved in ruling well. "He who rules over men must be just, ruling in the fear of God" (2 Samuel 23:3). Only a man expressing righteous character in consistently righteous acts could accomplish the great task of leading God's people. His experience taught him that only by constantly maintaining a sense of God's awesomeness could such character be maintained.

The sons of great kings do not always achieve the greatness of their fathers nor emulate the character that made their fathers great. While this concerned David, he understood his dynasty had only just begun. "Although my house is not so with God, yet He has made with me an everlasting covenant, ordered in all things and secure" (2 Samuel 23:5).

Despite the physical struggles, among others, which David dealt with in his final years, he continued to worship and serve the God who called him to the throne. He had seen a kingdom, which Saul had left in ruins, come together and expand to become a major force of power throughout the world. He had survived those who had sought to overtake his life or his power. He had experienced failure and frustration, but had dealt with them and seen success and victory. He had been present when his own son assumed his throne to become Israel's next king. "So David rested with his fathers, and was buried in the City of David. . . . Then Solomon sat on the throne of his father David; and his kingdom was firmly established" (1 Kings 2:10, 12).

GREAT LEADERS FINISH WELL

A great heritage can be both a blessing and a curse for the leader who follows. The one who follows a great leader inherits all that leader developed throughout a lifetime of service. The resources available at the beginning of the new reign are almost always greater than those available at the beginning of the previous one. But this also raises high expectations for the new leader. Many struggle in the shadow of a great leader, never quite able to measure up.

At the end of his life, David believed the best was yet to come. He knew much would be expected of Solomon and realized only God could provide the resources his son needed to lead. About the time of his coronation, David wrote a psalm in which he prayed for his son. He asked God to give his son the righteousness he believed was essential for leaders. Yet even as he prayed for his son, he revealed his confidence that Solomon would accomplish far more than he had been able to do.

"Give the king Your judgments, O God, and your righteousness to the king's Son. He will judge Your people with righteousness and Your poor with justice. The mountains will bring peace to the people and the little hills, by righteousness. He will bring justice to the poor of the people. He will save the children of the needy, and will break in pieces the oppressor. They shall fear You as long as the sun and moon endure, throughout all generations. He shall come down like rain upon the grass before mowing, like showers that water the earth. In His days the righteous shall flourish, and abundance of peace, until the moon is no more. He shall have dominion also from sea to sea, and from the River to the ends of the earth. Those who dwell in the wilderness will bow before Him, and His enemies will lick the dust" (Psalm 72:1-9).

GREAT LEADERS BELIEVE THE GREATEST LEADERS ARE YET TO COME

Although the Seventy-Second Psalm was written about Solomon, many Bible teachers believe the language of the psalm suggests that David was also looking beyond Solomon to Jesus, the Son of David (Matthew 1:1). "His name shall endure forever; His name shall continue as long as the sun, and all men shall be blessed in Him; all nations shall call Him blessed" (Psalm 72:17). In this context, the kingdom described in the psalm is that which will be established at the coming of Christ at the end of the age.

INDEED, THE GREATEST LEADER WILL COME AGAIN!

ENDNOTES

Chapter 1
1. A. W. Tozer, The Knowledge of the Holy: The Attributes of God: Their Meaning in the Christian Life (New York: Harper & Brothers, 1961), p. 10.

2. Tozer, The Knowledge of the Holy, p. 12.

3. Josephus, Antiquities of the Jews, vi, viii, 1, in Josephus: Complete Works, translated by William Whiston (Grand Rapids, MI: Kregel Publications, 1960), p. 133.

4. F. B. Meyer, David: Shepherd, Psalmist, King (Fort Washington, PA: Christian Literature Crusade, 1995), p. 20.

Chapter 2
1. F. B. Meyer, David: Shepherd, Psalmist, King (Fort Washington, PA: Christian Literature Crusade, 1995), pp. 34, 35.

2. Robert B. Greenblatt, Search the Scriptures (Illustrated): Modern Medicine and Biblical Personages (Lancashire, England: The Parthenon Press, 1985), p. 26.

Chapter 7
1. Frank Slaughter, David: Warrior and King: A Biblical Biography (New York: The World Publishing Company, 1962), pp. 294-296.

Chapter 9
1. F. B. Meyer, David: Shepherd, Psalmist, King (Fort Washington, Pennsylvania: Christian Literature Crusade, 1995), p. 201.

APPENDIX ONE

The Marks of a Great Leader
Drawn from the Life of a Great King

1. Great leaders grow while others stagnate.
2. Great leaders make decisions based on principles consistent with their personal core values.
3. Great leaders never forget their roots.

CHAPTER ONE
4. Great leaders know they are never truly alone.
5. Great leaders see and understand what others overlook.
6. Great leaders read great books and let them shape their values.
7. Great leaders humble themselves before a greater God.
8. Great leaders have a balanced perspective of who they truly are and could become.
9. Great leaders rise above the conditions into which they were born.
10. Great leaders learn from the failures of others.
11. Great leaders emerge for a great purpose.
12. Great leaders grow from within.
13. Great leaders serve by the power of the Spirit of God.

CHAPTER TWO
14. Great leaders value their personal relationship with God.
15. Great leaders pursue excellence in everything they do.
16. Great leaders use physical means to accomplish spiritual goals.
17. Great leaders are more committed to service than status.
18. Great leaders recognize challenging circumstances as significant opportunities.
19. Great leaders pursue causes worth pursuing.
20. Great leaders take on giants against whom they have no hope of winning, and win.

21. Great leaders make great victories the springboard for greater victories to come.

CHAPTER THREE

22. Great leaders earn credibility with the people they lead.
23. Great leaders recognize and honor the greatness of others.
24. Great leaders always run the risk of being misunderstood.
25. Great leaders are willing to adjust to serve where they can be most effective.
26. Great leaders walk with God regardless of where He takes them.
27. Great leaders exercise wisdom in their actions.
28. Great leaders pursue peace over conflict whenever possible.
29. Great leaders turn to God for help in the midst of desperate circumstances.
30. Great leaders consistently look for ways to inspire those who follow them.
31. Great leaders recognize God can change the inevitable for His glory and their good.
32. Great leaders turn to other great leaders for great counsel.
33. Great leaders experience great security while in the midst of God's will.

CHAPTER FOUR

34. Great leaders need great friends willing to stand with them regardless of the circumstances.
35. Great leaders have great relationships that shape who they become.
36. Great leaders surround themselves with friends willing to put themselves in harm's way in order to protect them.
37. Great leaders have friends who will make hard decisions for the benefit of their friend.
38. Great leaders rely on past victories for encouragement through a present crisis.
39. Great leaders find creative ways to resolve problems, even if the problem is of their own making.
40. Great leaders understand the value of solitude.

41. Great leaders push themselves and their followers to abandon the status quo for a higher standard.

42. Great leaders accept responsibility for the mistakes they make and problems they cause.

CHAPTER FIVE

43. Great leaders do not let personal problems distract them from the task at hand.

44. Great leaders are often the target of lesser men.

45. Great leaders are sometimes undervalued by those who owe them most.

46. Great leaders struggle with emotions common to all people.

47. Great leaders have great friends who encourage them in their faith in God.

48. Great leaders know when to refuse to take matters into their own hands.

49. Great leaders arise in the midst of transitional times.

50. Great leaders need wise counsel from many sources to avoid making unwise decisions.

51. Great leaders remain true to their personal values and act accordingly.

52. Great leaders use present opportunities to prepare for future endeavors.

53. Great leaders recognize the contributions of everyone involved, even those behind the frontlines.

CHAPTER SIX

54. Great leaders exhibit great generosity toward others.

55. Great leaders are consistently concerned for the welfare of those they are called to serve.

56. Great leaders exercise great justice, following principles above expedience.

57. Great leaders value truth and integrity.

58. Great leaders remember the very best of the very worst.

59. Great leaders are prepared to wait on God's timing.

60. Great leaders reach out with empathy to those who are hurting.

61. Great leaders do what needs to be done, even when they would rather not.

CHAPTER SEVEN

62. Great leaders allow their people time to change.

63. Great leaders earn the trust of those who follow them.

64. Great leaders understand the significance of great symbols.

65. Great leaders dream beyond their limits.

66. Great leaders find ways to make things happen.

67. Great leaders always remember what made them great in the first place.

68. Great leaders know the taste of failure.

69. Great leaders learn from their mistakes and adjust their lives accordingly.

70. Great leaders help their people remember great accomplishments.

CHAPTER EIGHT

71. Great leaders serve a purpose greater than themselves.

72. Great leaders sometimes face great disappointments.

73. Great leaders let God continually stretch their vision.

74. Great leaders always keep their humble status in perspective.

75. Great leaders remember their great heritage.

76. Great leaders give priority to bringing glory to God.

77. Great leaders believe God and act on the assurance He will honor His word.

78. Great leaders take time to plan and prepare for great undertakings.

79. Great leaders are great managers of human resources.

80. Great leaders promote great dreams that will outlive them.

81. Great leaders invite others to believe and be a part of their dreams.

82. Great leaders yield matters to God that are beyond their control.

CHAPTER NINE

83. Great leaders believe the promises of God and act accordingly.

84. Great leaders deal with the threat close to home before taking on more distant challenges.

85. Great leaders build on past victories to encourage others in the pursuit of new challenges.

86. Great leaders act to ensure potential enemies are not strong enough to do harm.

87. Great leaders are quick to acknowledge God's role in their great victories.

88. Great leaders establish a reputation others come to respect.

89. Great leaders remain aware of potential problems.

90. Great leaders delegate responsibility and authority to capable leaders.

91. Great leaders know not to use power to their own advantage.

92. Great leaders support the disenfranchised in society.

93. Great leaders model the character of the Greatest Leader.

94. Great leaders know the pain of having their motives misjudged by others.

CHAPTER TEN

95. Great leaders recognize that they are not perfect.

96. Great leaders make bad decisions when distracted from their primary task.

97. Great leaders make situations worse when they try to conceal their failures.

98. Great leaders live with the knowledge of their failures even when others are unaware.

99. Great leaders need courageous people who will hold them accountable for their actions.

100. Great leaders acknowledge and deal with their failure.

101. Great leaders live with the consequences of their failure.

102. Great leaders can be great again.

103. Great leaders lead by example, even when the example is negative.

104. Great leaders face more complex problems when they fail to address the simpler ones.

CHAPTER ELEVEN

105. Great leaders surround themselves with discerning followers.
106. Great leaders respond to wise rebuke regardless of its source.
107. Great leaders risk betrayal from those who are closest to them.
108. Great leaders maintain great flexibility in responding to situations.
109. Great leaders are not distracted from major problems by minor concerns.
110. Great leaders depend upon the loyalty of their closest advisors.
111. Great leaders are remembered and rewarded for their acts of kindness.
112. Great leaders see beyond dark times to bright new days.
113. Great leaders are confident of God's interest in their success.
114. Great leaders focus their thoughts to maintain a positive mental attitude.
115. Great leaders care for their adversaries.
116. Great leaders wisely balance justice and mercy.
117. Great leaders are challenged when they are perceived as weak.

CHAPTER TWELVE

118. Great leaders seek to correct past wrongs without compromising present commitments.
119. Great leaders recognize their limits and make necessary adjustments.
120. Great leaders view their influence as a gift from God.
121. Great leaders consider transparency to be a strong characteristic.
122. Great leaders are most vulnerable in their seasons of weakness.
123. Great leaders make great decisions when fully informed.
124. Great leaders communicate strong messages through their actions.
125. Great leaders pass on their insights to their successors.
126. Great leaders finish well.
127. Great leaders believe the greatest leaders are yet to come.

APPENDIX TWO

The Psalms of David in Chronological Context

The Psalms are a collection of 150 songs written over a period of a thousand years by various authors in different contexts. They were and continue to be widely used in the worship of God "to commemorate, to thank, and to praise the Lord God of Israel" (1 Chronicles 16:4). Among the various authors contributing to this collection, David was undoubtedly the most prolific writer of inspired psalms.

It is clear that the collection as it stands is not chronological. The oldest Psalm, the prayer of Moses, is the ninetieth psalm. Only fourteen psalms include superscriptions describing the historical context in which they were written (Psalms 3, 7, 18, 30, 34, 51, 52, 54, 56, 57, 59, 60, 63, 142). It is not surprising that there is some disagreement among biblical scholars concerning the chronological context of many psalms.

The following is the author's attempt to list those psalms attributed to David in their probable chronological context. Others have compiled similar lists in their biographies of David and commentaries on the psalms, with various conclusions being drawn. This listing has been prepared by comparing the contents of each psalm with various events in the life of David to identify a probable historical context.

The Early Years (6 Psalms)

1. David may have written Psalm 39 early in life, expressing his desire to live a godly life in spite of the home in which he was raised.
2. Psalm 19 appears to be David the shepherd's contemplation of the revelation of God in His created world and in the law he meditated on day and night.
3. Psalm 8 is also the product of one overwhelmed with the ways of God in His creation.
4. While Bible scholars disagree as to when David wrote

233

Psalm 23, his description of the Lord his Shepherd is obviously rooted in the context of his own work of shepherding his father's sheep.

5. The subject of Psalm 29 suggests the context of a violent thunderstorm, one of many David would have witnessed crossing the horizon as he shepherded his father's sheep.

6. Psalm 131 reflects a simple childlike faith typical of the young shepherd God sent Samuel to anoint as Israel's second king.

The Exile Years (24 Psalms)

7. The emphasis of Psalm 12 suggests it may have been written during David's conflict with Saul as his years as a fugitive began.

8. Psalm 11 is an expression of faith in God despite an obvious danger David faced, perhaps the danger of Saul's pursuit.

9. The superscription of Psalm 59 describes its historical context as the night when Saul's men surrounded David's house to arrest and kill him.

10. The superscription of Psalm 7 places this psalm in the exile years as he was being pursued by one of Saul's relatives, Cush, a Benjamite.

11. Psalm 25, an acrostic psalm, describes conditions similar to David's experience during the exile years.

12. The superscription over Psalm 56 describes the historical context as being when the Philistines captured David in Gath as he ran from Saul.

13. The superscription above Psalm 34 attributes this psalm to the same situation, as he pretended madness before Abimelech to escape.

14. The superscription over Psalm 142 describes a historical context of David being in the cave, probably the Cave of Adullam.

15. The superscription of Psalm 57 identifies its historical context as being when David fled from Saul into the cave,

probably the Cave of Adullam.

16. Psalm 141 was written during an intense trial in the life of David, perhaps during his fugitive years in which Saul was pursuing him.

17. In Psalm 64, David prays those plotting against him will fail, a prayer that was surely typical of David's prayers during his exile.

18. Likewise, Psalm 35 is David's cry of distress over being falsely accused, suggesting a historical context of the exile years.

19. The superscription over Psalm 52 identifies the context as being when Doeg the Edomite told Saul David had gone to the house of Ahimelech, resulting in the death of the priests at Nob.

20. Psalm 109 is an imprecatory prayer of David and may express his feelings toward his enemies during his exile years.

21. Psalm 31 is a blending of laments as David reflects on his problems and praises as he acknowledges God's provision, conditions which existed during the exile years.

22. The repeated question, "How long?" in Psalm 13 suggests this psalm was written during the exile years.

23. Psalm 22 describes the desperation of David during his exile years in such vivid detail that it was used by Christ to describe the agony of the cross.

24. David probably wrote Psalm 10 at a low point during his exile when he was so discouraged he felt abandoned by God.

25. Psalm 9 and Psalm 10 form an acrostic, suggesting they were written at or about the same time.

26. Psalm 17 is one of three "prayers of David," this one apparently written during his exile years as he fled from Saul.

27. The superscription of Psalm 54 places its context as being when the Ziphites betrayed David, telling Saul of his location.

28.   Psalm 69 is yet another description of the suffering David probably experienced during his years of exile.

29.   Psalm 16 was written while David still struggled with his enemies but was becoming increasingly confident of better days ahead.

30.   Psalm 27 is a strong affirmation of faith probably written toward the end of David's exile as he reflected back on God's faithfulness over the years.

The Regal Years (28 Psalms)

31.   Psalm 124 may have been written early in David's reign as he reflects on conditions that threatened his survival during the exile.

32-35. Psalms 96 through 99 are enthronement psalms linked together with the phrase "the Lord reigns" and may have been written shortly after David assumed the throne of Judah.

36.   Psalm 15 may have been written during David's reign over Judah as it references "the Lord's throne." It was written at a time when David felt endangered, perhaps during the civil war between Judah and Israel.

37.   Psalm 28 may have been another prayer written by David during the civil war years in which he prays for the safety of his people.

38.   Psalm 108 is a blending of parts of Psalms 57 and 60 and may have been arranged to celebrate the uniting of the kingdom of Israel following the seven-year civil war.

39.   Psalm 101 appears to be David's commitment to a godly rule as king, probably written when he assumed the throne of Israel.

40.   The superscription of Psalm 30 suggests it was written for the dedication of the house of David in his new capital, Jerusalem.

41.   Psalm 145 is the only psalm described as a praise psalm in its superscription, suggesting David may have written it for use as the Ark of the Covenant was brought to Jerusalem.

42.   Psalm 118 is a song of thanksgiving and praise and may have been written as part of the celebration for the arrival of the ark in Jerusalem.

43.   Most Bible teachers agree Psalm 68 was written about the time the ark was moved to Jerusalem.

44.   Psalm 122 celebrates the worship of God in "the house of the Lord" and may have been written shortly after the Tabernacle had been established in Jerusalem.

45.   Psalm 138 is a personal song of praise that looks forward to the universal praise of God and may have been written soon after the ark arrived in Jerusalem.

46.   Psalm 2 was apparently written in the midst of military conflicts and speaks also of the spiritual conflicts faced by Christians.

47.   David may have written Psalm 14 during a conflict with a nation that denied the validity of the Lord God of Israel.

48.   Psalm 53 is similar to Psalm 14, suggesting they may have been written about the same time.

49.   The content of Psalm 5 suggests it was written during the phase of David's reign when he was expanding Israel's territory through military conflict.

50.   Psalm 20 is a prayer for the king as he prepares to lead his people into battle, suggesting it was written during David's years of expanding the kingdom.

51.   Psalm 21 appears to be the king's response to the people's prayer in Psalm 20, suggesting they were written about the same time.

52.   The superscription of Psalm 60 identifies its historical context as being when he fought against Mesopotamia and Syria of Zobah and Joab returned and killed twelve thousand Edomites in the Valley of Salt.

53.   One of the royal psalms, Psalm 93 celebrates God's rule over Israel during both David's reign and the kingdom to come.

54.   Although it has no specific reference to David's rule, Psalm

110 is a messianic psalm celebrating God's coming rule.

55. Psalm 95 is a celebration of God's rule over Israel suggesting a context in which the throne was well established in Israel.

56. Psalm 18 was apparently written during David's peaceful years as king as the superscription describes when the Lord delivered David from all his enemies, including Saul.

57. Psalm 24 celebrates God's ownership over all His creation and may have been written as David completed his conquests and expanded Israel's boundaries.

58. Psalm 105 is apparently David's only historical psalm and may have been written for use in the worship services of the Tabernacle.

The Bathsheba Affair (9 Psalms)

59. Psalm 45 is a wedding psalm and may have been written for use at David's marriage to Bathsheba.

60. Although probably written after his encounter with Nathan, Psalm 32 describes David's agony about his sin with Bathsheba during the period when he thought he had gotten away with it.

61. The superscription over Psalm 51 identifies it as one written when Nathan the prophet confronted David about Bathsheba.

62. Psalm 41 was written during a time when David struggled about the physical consequences of his sin with Bathsheba.

63. Psalm 38 vividly describes the kind of physical illness David experienced in the aftermath of his affair with Bathsheba.

64. Psalm 6 expresses the same sense of guilt and physical conditions described in other psalms written about the time of David's affair with Bathsheba.

65. Psalm 139 celebrates the greatness of God, a knowledge of God that may have grown out of David's struggle during the Bathsheba affair.

66. Psalm 103 is a song of thanksgiving for many things

including the forgiveness of sins, and may have been written out of David's sense of forgiveness for his sin with Bathsheba.

67. Psalm 106 is a national lament and may have been written as part of the nation's grieving process over increased military conflict, a consequence of David's sin with Bathsheba.

The Absalom Rebellion (14 Psalms)

68. The superscription of Psalm 3 identifies it as a psalm written when he fled from his son Absalom.

69. Psalm 4 was written as an evening prayer, probably in the time of David's exile during Absalom's rebellion.

70. Although conditions in Psalm 61 may reflect earlier battles, his references to past victories and the king's survival suggest David may have written it during Absalom's revolt.

71. The superscription of Psalm 63 describes its context as being when David was in the wilderness of Judah, perhaps during Absalom's rebellion.

72. David wrote Psalm 55 as he endured the consequences of Ahithophel's betrayal during Absalom's rebellion.

73. Psalm 26 was written at a time when David felt he had been falsely accused, a condition that existed during Absalom's rebellion.

74. Psalm 140 was written at a time when David sensed a real threat from his enemies, perhaps during Absalom's rebellion.

75. In Psalm 58, David speaks against unjust judges and counselors, perhaps thinking of specific counselors who had betrayed him during Absalom's rebellion.

76. Psalm 143 was likewise written during a time when his enemies threatened David, as was the case in Absalom's rebellion.

77. Psalm 39 appears to have been written at a confusing time in David's life, causing great emotional stress, perhaps during Absalom's rebellion.

78. Psalm 62 is a psalm of confidence that may have been penned by David when he learned Ahithophel's advice to

Absalom had been rejected.

79. Psalm 40 includes the mix of lament and thanksgiving that must have gripped David when he learned Absalom's revolt was over but his son had died.

80. Psalm 70 was apparently detached from the final verses of Psalm 40, suggesting they were written at the same time.

81. Psalm 36 describes insights into God's forgiveness of sin, which David may have learned or been reminded of during Absalom's rebellion.

The Final Years of David (8 Psalms)

82. If written by David, Psalm 133 may have been written to celebrate the reunification of the kingdom following Absalom's revolt.

83. Psalm 37 is a psalm of confidence written in David's latter years as he reflects on God's faithfulness over the years.

84. Psalm 65 is a thanksgiving psalm celebrating the harvest and may have been written by David toward the end of his reign.

85. Psalm 144 is a royal psalm probably compiled by David from several of his earlier psalms late in his reign.

86. Psalm 86 is described as a prayer of David that may have been prayed later in David's life when his body began to fail him.

87. David apparently wrote Psalm 72 for use at his son Solomon's coronation as his successor and Israel's third king.

88. Although it may have been written at various times during David's life, Psalm 119 could have been written to encourage his sons and successors to honor God's word throughout their reigns.

89. Although first in the Psalter, Psalm 1 may have been written late in David's life as a testimony to God's blessing.